Social Care Practice in Ireland:
An Integrated Perspective

Social Care Practice in Ireland: An Integrated Perspective

Celesta McCann James, Áine de Róiste
and John McHugh

GILL EDUCATION

Gill Education
Hume Avenue
Park West
Dublin 12

www.gilleducation.ie

Gill Education is an imprint of M.H. Gill & Co.

978 07171 4509 6

Index compiled by Rachel Pierce, Verba Editing House Print
origination in Ireland by Carole Lynch

The paper used in this book is made from the wood pulp
of managed forests. For every tree felled, at least one tree
is planted, thereby renewing natural resources.

A CIP catalogue record for this book is available
from the British Library.

Contents

PART THREE: ETHICS

Introduction

This book isn't finished! It is waiting for the reader to engage in discussion and purposeful conversation about the presented themes, topics and scenarios of social care practice. The practice scenarios included invite the student to engage actively rather than passively with theoretical coursework. The overall aim of the book is to promote a sense of ownership on the part of the student regarding their own professional development as they journey towards professional qualification. Hartley (2005) puts it well when he says: 'Journeying, with its sense of setting off, building, constructing, changing, and arriving, includes all the important conceptual ingredients to generate powerful experiential learning' (p. 7).

The famous Irish middle-distance runner, Catriona McKiernan, was interviewed about how her career as a runner developed. She spoke about how her natural ability and dedication had brought her success on a national stage. Her potential to move onto the international stage was obvious. Taking this step involved a new, more 'professional' approach to training and preparation. She had always enjoyed training which usually consisted of long, gruelling runs around her local golf course. Little attention was given to anything other than her overall fitness level. Her new training regime, however, took an entirely different approach, one that broke down the elements of training for competitive running into its component parts – fitness, movement, diet, mental attitude, use of different muscles and so on. For a while her new knowledge and consciousness about running had a negative impact on her race times. Her natural flow was being curtailed as she became more conscious of what she was doing. However, over time the benefits began to be seen. She could now reflect and discuss with her trainer what went well – or not so well – in a race, and then work on specific improvements. She could look ahead to races and run to different tactical plans. The whole running experience was now more enjoyable again, but, more than that, Catriona was in control of herself as a runner and achieving consistently on the world stage. Her potential was being realised.

Many students of social care are motivated by a deep concern for the welfare of vulnerable and/or dependent people. To their academic programmes they bring strong caring abilities and 'helping skills' often practised in non-professional settings. Their challenge is to bring this potential to a professional level. This involves becoming more conscious of the 'what', 'why' and 'how' of our actions. 'To achieve this perspective, individuals must come to an understanding of their own behaviour; they must develop a conscious awareness of their own actions and effects and the ideas or theories-in-use that shape their action strategies' (Osterman and Kottkamp 1993 in Bennet et al. 1994, p. 46). 'Reflective practice' (Schön, 1983; Kolb, 1984; Bolton, 2005) is the term used to describe how learning in the professional context is underpinned by reflection, contemplation and experiment. Schön (1983) distinguished between 'reflection-in-action' and 'reflection-on-action': both are essential to the reflective social care practitioner. The challenge for students of social care (and their lecturers) is to develop reflective practice skills *prior to* professional practice. 'The situations of practice are not problems to be solved but problematic situations characterised by uncertainty, disorder and indeterminacy' (Schön, 1983, p. 16). So how does one learn to be a social care professional? How does one teach those wishing to become social care professionals?

Moore (1970) offers some hope:

> If every professional problem were in all respects unique, solutions would be at best accidental, and therefore have nothing to do with expert knowledge. What we are suggesting, on the contrary, is that there are sufficient uniformities in problems and in devices for solving them to qualify the solvers as professionals...
>
> (p. 56)

Our experience in working with students brought us to the conclusion that whilst students did make efforts to avail of the opportunities in practice placement to link theory and practice, to develop skills, and to become aware of their professional selves, their learning seemed to be placement-specific; their development towards professional practice was not being built on over time as they moved to new placement or work settings. There may be several reasons for this: traditional teaching and learning models (namely technical rationality) still dominate; class sizes and course structures combine to reduce opportunities for reflection and exploration; a limited view of what the social care professional role is or can be on the part of all involved in the teaching and learning process, and in some cases on a wider societal level; or underdeveloped reflective practice skills. It is this last reason that prompted us to write this book. Certainly, practical work-placements that are supported by clear learning plans and good-quality supervision can and do help develop these skills in students. It is our contention, however, that the development of reflective practice skills can and must be central to the whole social care learning/training experience. In other words, it is not enough for students to acquire knowledge; they must develop skills to put their knowledge to use.

Osterman and Kottkamp (1993) pose some interesting questions: 'If the purpose of reflective practice is to enhance awareness of our own thoughts and action, as a means of professional growth, how do we begin this process of reflection? How do we begin to develop a critical awareness about our own professional practice? Where do we start?' (p. 47). Our answer is, 'right here, right now, through meaningful dialogue and purposeful conversation'.

In creating a framework for discussion, we have identified themes relating to social care practice: Inclusion, Ethics and Rights. Within each theme, specific topics are explored in relation to case scenarios from real-life practice situations (see Table 1.1).

Table 1.1

Themes	Inclusion	Rights	Ethics
Practice Scenario Topic	Cultural diversity	Advocacy	Personal/ Professional boundaries
Context	*Neighbourhood Youth Project*	*Homeless Agency*	*Drug Treatment Centre*
Practice Scenario Topic	Access and Empowerment	Interdisciplinary work	Confidentiality
Context	*Training Centre*	*Community Childcare*	*Residential Care*
Practice Scenario Topic	Promoting independent living	Partnership approach	Self: reflective practice
Context	*Day Care Centre for Older People*	*Family Resource Centre*	*Community Mental Health*

This book is divided into three themed sections with an illustrative practice scenario from a different social care context. Each scenario forms the basis of an individual chapter that contains the following:

1. A presentation of the Irish context and background of the social issue in question, service provision and service user profile.
2. Presentation of the practice scenario.
3. Sociological perspective (with focus on one or two key theories and/or relevant concepts).
4. Psychological perspective (with focus on one or two key theories and/or relevant concepts).
5. Practice perspective (supported by focused interviews on practice scenarios from service-user and/or service-provider perspectives).

Each topic is discussed in turn from the perspective of sociology, psychology and practice skills. These discussions are the beginning of exploration, dialogue and conversation. Their starting point is to consider 'How can our knowledge and understanding of psychology (or practice skills or sociology) inform our thinking and develop our professional competence in relation to this topic?' The scenarios themselves are just that – snapshots in time, providing a window into the sometimes confused, imperfect and complex world of social care practice. Reading each scenario, the student begins a dialogue with peers and professionals about the issues raised by the topic. The dialogue that follows each scenario is the beginning of conversation. The reader will notice that, in some cases, conversation has already begun – in the practice perspectives, both service-providers and service-users were asked to comment on the scenarios presented. Their contributions are sometimes surprising, sometimes challenging and always relevant.

Figure 1.1 illustrates Kolb's (1984) Experimental Learning Cycle. On it we have super-imposed the pre-experiential learning cycle. By gaining experience in the form of the case scenarios the student can follow the same learning cycle – 'a dialogue of thinking and doing through which I become more skilful' (Schön, 1987).

This approach challenges traditional teaching and learning methodologies that dominate many undergraduate educational experiences. We are not calling for a complete overthrow of the existing model: it is vital, however, that space be created, recognised and valued within social care programmes that allows students to explore how discrete modules, theories and skill-sets relate to each other and to their journey of professional development; they need to be afforded a space to create their own integrated perspective.

Figure 1.1

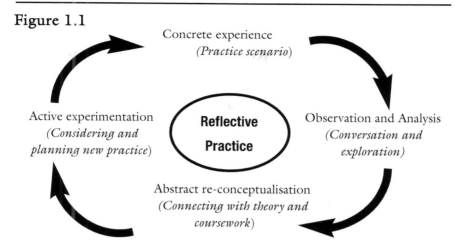

There are many ways to use this book. Any chapter or even part of a chapter may be used to generate reflective discussion as an in-class exercise or tutorial work; it may also be useful in placement preparation to illustrate the relationship between theory and practice. A useful model in promoting an integrated perspective is that of the World Café, an innovative yet simple methodology for hosting conversations about questions that matter – like those raised by the practice scenarios. These conversations will link up and build upon each other as people move between groups, cross-pollinate ideas, revise their questions and discover new insights into the issues at play. Detailed information on the world café methodology and approach can be found at www.theworldcafe.com. In brief, the general flow is as follows:

1. Groups of four to five are seated at café-style tables. Paper tablecloths and markers or crayons allow the group write or draw their ideas and questions.
2. Progressive 'rounds' of conversation flow from questions aimed at focusing the discussion.
3. At the end of each 'round', one person remains at the table as 'host' while the other members move to other tables as ambassadors of the ideas and insights of their table.
4. The table host shares the key insights and ideas from that table with the new table members as the new round of conversations begin.
5. Having moved through the rounds (usually three or four), the group is allowed some time for a whole-group harvest of the conversations.

(www.theworldcafe.com)

This book is organised into nine chapters, each one focusing on a distinct topic. It is important to point out that the topic of a particular chapter is not exclusive to the setting illustrated in the accompanying practice scenario. The skills identified and themes discussed are transferable between chapters, and indeed to settings beyond this text. As the discussions unfold through the chapters it is hoped that the reader will develop a clearer insight into professional social care work – the range of skills involved; the theoretical framework that underpins and informs it; and the personal involvement of the 'professional self' in practice that is based on close working relationships. In promoting an integrated perspective based on reflective practice, we hope that social care students and workers will be able to think more clearly about their profession and ultimately work more effectively with the people who use their services.

PART ONE

INCLUSION

Inclusion: An Irish Context

Inclusive practice refers to commitment and support for social inclusion that allows individuals and groups to prosper. Anchored in Aristotle's ethics, social inclusion has become an objective of European and Irish legislation. In the context of social care, practice strives to ensure that no individuals or groups are disenfranchised, excluded or discriminated against. Students and care practitioners can facilitate inclusive practice by promoting social and structural changes to accommodate service users in a more comprehensive manner. Assisting service users to participate in decision-making that affects their lives is central to this goal. Student training in inclusive practice also involves recognising the abilities and positive attributes of service users, identifying their strengths as well as sources of resilience. In addition, training that helps students to see and encourage the expression of the service users' own unique personal perspectives and experiences of the world merits attention. Consequently, social care training develops skills in listening and hearing phenomenologically as well as considering how people experience their own personal reality. 'Listening phenomenologically can enable us to enter into a client's world and perhaps gain some sense of what that world is really like' (Kennefick, 2006, p. 260).

A popular inclusion framework used in Western societies is one that facilitates social inclusion through employment. This view is one that accepts current structures, institutions and practices in society and expects that people will be incorporated into existing social supports driven largely by economic labour market activity that produces acceptable behaviour and a reproduction of cultural values (Moran, 2006). Rather than challenging exclusion, this view fails to acknowledge the inequalities (e.g. low pay, job insecurity, low status and low benefits) that permeate the employment sector. In addition, it undermines the legitimacy of unpaid work in voluntary areas as well as in community and domestic spheres. As a result, social concerns are typically addressed through economic activity, leaving many workers to experience material deprivation and socio-political isolation. (Levitas, 2005; Lynch et al., 2006).

A second view of exclusion is one that defines the excluded in society as morally wanting. It points the finger at the feet of the poor and social outcasts rather than at the structure of society. This view argues against benefits for the disadvantaged, claiming that they cause dependency and weakened morality. The flawed social structure is not acknowledged but, rather, the excluded are here seen to be responsible for their own marginalisation and considered to pose a risk to a cohesive, viable society (see, for example, Murray, 2006).

A third explanation of social exclusion is one that Levitas (2005) labels as 'redistributionist'. It suggests that social exclusion is caused by poverty, and claims that if society reduces its levels of poverty through the redistribution of resources and power (e.g. by increasing benefits), it will minimalise exclusion. Under this model, all members of society participate fully in economic, political, social and cultural activities. Resources and power are redistributed in such a way so as to ensure that everyone is represented equally and that all members of society are guaranteed parity and inclusive participation.

In 2007, the Irish government published its 'National Action Plan for Social Inclusion 2007–2016' (Government Publications, 2007). The plan states that due to substantial progress in income support over recent years, delivery of services and support for quality employment has been increased. As outlined in the social integration and redistribution models above, the government plan of action focuses on reducing and/or eliminating consistent poverty by targeting the role of employment, income supports (e.g. minimum wage, tax reform, flexible social welfare) and community participation for vulnerable individuals and groups, including children, older people and people with disabilities. The plan also agrees that disadvantaged areas are in need of increased social capital and integration. A key to monitoring the outcomes of these stated goals lies in the ability of government departments, agencies and other organisations to work together, using a multi-policy approach. Walsh and colleagues (1998) argue previously that local initiatives and policy-making may be encouraged, but the retention of control, supply of funding and policy direction remains with central government, leaving a socio-economic contradiction. A balanced approach is therefore needed, one that will enhance local resources, promote social capital and build local consensus and shared decision-making.

CULTURAL DIVERSITY AND INCLUSION

Racism has been identified by social science professions as a powerful component of social and cultural exclusion in society. With particular reference to refugees and asylum seekers, challenges associated with dislocation, power and discrimination are regularly identified. Even more specific are the issues faced by unaccompanied children: an unaccompanied minor is a child who has arrived seeking asylum but without any parental or family support. They are vulnerable to violence, have little if any voice and face great difficulty accessing services. Many of these children have moved from their countries of origin because of violence or abuse, carry the emotional scars of their past, and now find themselves confronting discrimination and racism in Ireland while facing the added challenge of integrating into a new culture (ISPCC, 2005).

The Irish Refugee Council highlights that unaccompanied minors are often 'invisible' due to the fact that fewer than 5 per cent are identified at the port of entry. This suggests that many do not come to the attention of the authorities as individuals seeking asylum. Rather, unaccompanied minors may have been trafficked in prostitution or abused in other ways (e.g. child slavery). In her research, Conroy (2003) found that many unaccompanied children had been sexually abused before arriving in Ireland and others have been removed by unauthorised adults from their accommodation and recorded as missing. Very often, unaccompanied minors are treated as older than their years, under an inaccurate presumption that they are more resilient than other children their age. Barnardos (2000), the Children's Rights Alliance (2008), the Irish Society for the Prevention of Cruelty to Children (2005) and the Irish Refugee Council (Mooten, 2006) have argued for the need for a child-friendly approach to the asylum system with recognition given to the likelihood of these children having experienced, amongst other possibilities, forced conscription as child soldiers, female genital mutilation and child labour. The Health Service Executive (HSE) has identified unaccompanied minors as a group that needs specifically targeted services.

Unaccompanied minors can apply for asylum on the recommendation of the HSE, but for those who do not, their status is unclear and their rights are less clear still. Like other social service users, unaccompanied minors need social support in the areas of communication, assessment, resources, advocacy and counselling. In addition, there are huge concerns regarding their lack of inclusion with local communities. Care providers can assist such minors by establishing local links to educational programmes, community associations and centres and family networks.

DISABILITY AND INCLUSION

In the past, individuals with a disability were viewed as a problem and in need of treatment or a cure. This medical model caused alienation and placed the challenge of impairment upon individuals rather than on society. As a result, services concentrated on protection and rehabilitation, frequently moving people with disabilities from ordinary life settings to institutional care. This approach also attempted to 'compensate' people for what was 'wrong' with their bodies by providing targeted benefits and/or segregated special services (Enable Ireland, 2008). Consequently, by internalising this view of themselves, individuals with impairments sometimes accepted discrimination and subsequently failed to challenge the social structures that put them at a disadvantage.

Since the 1970s, the disability movement has sought to establish a social model that views the position of disabled people and the discrimination against them as 'socially created'. This model holds that impairments should not prevent people from having a reasonable standard of living, nor should they make an individual less suitable to participate in society. Rather, it sees prejudicial attitudes and discriminating social environments as impediments to people's lives (Combat Poverty Agency, 2005). Enable Ireland (2008) recognises that, in reality, most problems experienced by individuals are not caused by their impairments, but by the way that society is organised. Therefore, if individuals with impairments are to be facilitated to engage in society, society must remove the barriers that prevent them from participating. Equal rights and non-discriminatory practice, both in legislation and in social practices, help to elevate the way that individuals see themselves, as well as the way that they are seen by others. Recent legislation has facilitated rights-based, mainstream policies for individuals and communities who previously experienced many forms of social exclusion.

There is evidence of an increase in the number of intellectually disabled people in Ireland and this is largely viewed as a result of an increase in the general population, but is also due to an increase in the lifespan of the intellectually disabled (Kelly et al., 2007). Improved health and well-being, the control of infectious diseases, the move to community living, improved nutrition, and the quality of health care services can be credited for this increased longevity. Subsequently, health providers face new challenges as care facilities and therapeutic support services are in greater demand. Although changes are slow in coming, disability groups are using models of advocacy to increase their social and political presence in Irish society. Even with this trend, however, employers, service providers and policy makers need to work continually towards a society where the experience of disability is no longer linked to exclusion and poverty.

OLDER PEOPLE AND INCLUSION

The aged are not a uniform category in Ireland and no single definition of 'old age' or the 'elderly' can rightly identify or represent the identities, experiences and life goals of our older population. Considering them as a single group is too simplistic because knowledge and perceptions of old age are as varied as the number of individuals involved. Because defining and measuring old age as a social category is challenging, so too is the formation of social policies and structures that will successfully identify their diverse needs and facilitate positive action.

In the past, older people in Ireland have been viewed as a group within the larger population in need of 'treatment'. Ageing was largely identified as a physical process in which older people were seen as comfortable, independent pensioners or alternatively as being in the sole care of their extended family. Public attention and social policy focused upon government medical provision when necessary, and psychological and sociological intervention was left to poorly funded non-governmental organisations. While it may be broadly accepted that medical and social models are both valid and appropriate frameworks for elder care, the starting place for evaluating older people in Irish society should not presume that they are all sick or frail. Some older people may experience a chronic illness but, even for them, such a condition is only part of who they are. They are also emotional, psychological and social beings with needs and entitlements that demand and deserve consideration just like any other group of individuals in a population.

In 1981, the Minister for Health set out terms of reference that looked at existing planning and provision services for the older population of Ireland. It was envisaged that as a result of analysing existing practices and conducting appropriate research, recommendations would come forward to meet the needs of the aged. A series of National Councils were formed to promote the social inclusion of older people in Irish society, and social care and provision for the aged became a main theme of health service considerations. (For recent examples of discussions and recommendations, see Ruddle et al., 1997 and the National Council on Ageing and Older People, 2004.) The NCAOP (2005) has developed more recently a clear outline of objectives that proposes constructive guidelines for an age-friendly society. Some of the objectives do not appear to be all too different from those associated with social care education and practice; for example, anti-ageist attitudes, integration, needs-focused, person-centred provision, flexibility, empowerment and partnership.

— —

In considering the three scenarios that follow, key social care objectives are linked with psychological issues such as independent living, loneliness, social isolation, health and well-being. Sociological issues are also presented that integrate fundamental concepts such as stratification, discrimination, ageism and social participation. Essential to each case are the perspectives of social care service-providers and service-users. These have been drawn from interviews with the two groups, conducted to allow for their meaningful contribution to the discussion. The blend of themes and perspectives covered allows the reader an opportunity to explore how ethnicity, disability and age intersect with inclusion and social care frameworks. The core objective of the chapters within this theme is to allow readers to consider ways in which a fair and inclusive society can be facilitated for service users. Students and practitioners are challenged to consider whether present structures offer empowering and rewarding opportunities for service-users or if they contribute to vulnerability that results in psychological inhibition and social withdrawal.

– 1 –
Cultural Diversity

- There are currently 188 new nationalities represented in Ireland (Central Statistics Office, 2006).
- Over 4,500 unaccompanied minors (also referred to as 'separated children') have arrived in Ireland over recent years seeking asylum and the majority of these are adolescent children of 16–17 years of age (ISPCC, 2005).
- The main countries of origin of unaccompanied minors have been Somalia, Afghanistan and Nigeria, with reasons for leaving their home country including political and civil conflicts and natural disasters (Mooten, 2006).
- Approximately half of unaccompanied minors are reunited with their biological families, and the remainder are most often placed in care, especially hostel care (Mooten, 2006).

Practice Scenario 1
Setting – Community Youth Project

Claire has just begun working in a youth project that includes young people from the local residential community. Over the past four years, the project has been receiving numbers of young unaccompanied minors seeking asylum. At the moment, in addition to the four Irish teens in the project, there are two teenagers from Nigeria, one from Afghanistan and one from Moldova. Along with the other staff, Claire would like to help these young people to mix more with the other teenagers rather than keep so much to themselves and their fellow nationals.

Karim, the teenager from Afghanistan, enjoys fishing, as do three of the four Irish boys. Despite Claire's encouragement and offers from other members of staff, Karim has never joined any of the fishing outings organised by the project. Claire even heard one of the Irish boys, Daniel, invite Karim to the next Saturday fishing trip, but Karim, looking at some of his other friends, offered an excuse and said he couldn't be bothered. On a trip to a shop one day, Claire saw some of the Nigerian teenagers being teased by some of the local Irish teens, including some who attend the project. When Claire asked them about it they didn't want to talk about it.

Concerned with what she has heard and witnessed, Claire seeks to learn more about Karim and some of the other service-users of the youth project. She learns that Karim and the other boys rely on independent and unsupervised lodging because they are presently living in a self-catering, privately managed hostel, set up by the Health Service Executive as an interim care accommodation. Karim is one of over twenty teenagers living in the B&B and he is without adequate resources, support or any long-term care plan.

With this information, Claire reports to her colleagues at the project that she feels exclusion from some of the planned activities is only an indication of further social and psychological exclusion (e.g. teasing and bullying) that some of the teens are experiencing in the community. The project team agrees that an intervention plan is urgent.

For further consideration...

How can Claire facilitate the following?
- Inclusion of and respect for 'difference'
- Integration of multicultural values and norms
- Tolerance, appreciation and preservation of cultural identities
- Policy change within the community youth project

Review the scenario and perspectives **below** *and try to name other unfamiliar skills that might become part of the professional Social Care Toolkit.*

SOCIOLOGICAL PERSPECTIVE

Claire has correctly identified core issues facing the teens who have arrived in Ireland from other countries. Through no fault of their own, the teens are experiencing social difficulties at a number of different levels. It is likely that they are unfamiliar with Irish culture, values and expected behaviour (i.e. norms) and they may feel uncomfortable with their experience of Irish teen language, behaviour and ways of socialising. Such circumstances can lead to broad forms of social exclusion. Social exclusion may occur when an individual or group is 'cut off' from full involvement in society or when they find that they are restricted in terms of social contacts and supports.

Social exclusion is sometimes associated with poverty or marginalisation resulting from economic barriers, but it may also result from social processes or individual choices that lead to isolation and further social problems.

Giddens (2001) suggests that 'Social exclusion can result from people excluding themselves from aspects of mainstream society. Individuals can choose to drop out ...' Being one of only a few Afghans in the community and socially inexperienced in Ireland, Karim has not had an opportunity to represent his views or priorities regarding activities in the youth project. He has not contributed to decisions or plans, nor has he voiced any of the concerns that he and his friends have about what the teens might organise. Although Karim's physical and economic needs are being met by the Health Service Executive, and as a part if the youth project he is given opportunities to participate in the community, he is still experiencing significant forms of social disadvantage. Karim and his friends are struggling to integrate within the community youth project and are also the targets of discriminating and prejudicial comments in the wider community.

As a project worker focusing upon the needs of a number of teens from varying social backgrounds, Claire recognises from her professional training that there is often difficulty in groups when social values are not shared across the group. Her challenge is to identify the teens' existing social values and how those values influence Karim and his peers' ability to participate in the activities organised by the youth project. It occurs to Claire that up to this point, all of the activities that have been organised and planned in the project have been initiated either by members of staff or by Irish teens who live in the community. She decides that in order to include Karim and his peers in the project, there needs to be a structure that facilitates their meaningful social participation and decision-making. Claire decides to raise this with Karim and the other teens, in order to allow them to identify their feelings and priority objectives on this issue. Agencies such as the Irish Society for the Prevention of Cruelty to Children (2005) make the point that children are sometimes viewed as passive participants in society. They are seldom encouraged to participate actively in the social structures that affect their lives (e.g. education, health and justice). Rather, children are defined as belonging to adults or simply as components of a family. Such views lessen children's worth and significance and decrease their opportunity to share or influence society's values and ideologies. In order to change this diminished position, effective advocacy is needed as well as a commitment on the part of service providers to represent the voices, experiences and needs of children. One way of facilitating participation in the scenario above is by introducing familiar foods, music and rituals from Karim's culture. Based on interviews with a small sample of separated children, Veki (2003) found that some children preferred to cook their own culture's food. Others, however, reported that hostels lacked appropriate facilities. At present, the majority of separated children do not reside in children's care centres but in privately managed hostel accommodation. Of greater concern is the fact that these hostels and residential centres occupied by separated children are not subject to inspection by the Irish Social Service Inspectorate (McCann James, 2005; Mooten, 2006).

Claire and other care staff could better care for separated children by learning about their different cultures, special cultural days and religious events. In addition, cultural games and sports might help in small ways to alleviate the distress and 'strangeness' separated children experience when living in another culture. Equally, helping such children understand Irish norms and ways of life can assist them to understand and feel more as if they belong in Irish society. Inclusion policies involving separated children assist towards this goal and are in place in some existing children's services.

Another significant component aiding inclusion is that of language interpretation and support services. Each of these play a crucial role for both children and care staff. Service programmes that befriend and mentor, such as the Big Brother-Big Sister programme, assist children and foster a sense of belonging and social integration. Attendance at school is also beneficial in normalising children's lives and help their integration into society by providing them with a sense of purpose and structure (Mooten, 2006). Preparatory programmes are still needed, however, to help children from other cultures and background adjust to Irish schools and access the full academic and social curriculum, as some of them may never have had any experience of formal education (Wanzenböck, 2006).

Claire is also faced with evidence of racism amongst the teens in the local community. She has heard and seen derogatory actions by Irish teens towards the two Nigerian teens. Racism is seen to exist when an attitude or behaviour (either intentional or unintentional) is disadvantaging the social position of a specific group (McCann James, 2005). It often takes the form of group closure where social boundaries are formed and then used to exclude an individual or group from a form of power or social standing. At other times, racism exists because groups are believed to be 'inferior' because of a biological or cultural difference. If Karim's lack of social participation was rare or occasional, Claire might assess it differently. Instead, the reluctance to participate in the fishing trip and other organised outings has demonstrated that the 'non-Irish' teens are being socially deprived *as a group* and perhaps being subjected to feelings of inferiority and/or marginalisation.

Social inclusion for minors like Karim includes policy action that does not tolerate any form of discrimination or exclusion. It views all children as active participants in the social structures that impact their new lives in Ireland. A key part of achieving this is a multidisciplinary approach that provides specialist services and 24-hour care for unaccompanied children, resources that support family and/or community reunification and access to educational and vocational studies. By implementing these and other recommendations, unaccompanied children in Ireland will be more visible and thereby more likely to experience a safe and meaningful childhood that values their physical, emotional and social lives.

Sociological issues highlighted in this practice scenario include: inclusion, respect for 'difference', integration of values and norms, tolerance, preservation of cultural identities, social exclusion, marginalisation, discrimination, prejudice, and group deprivation.

PSYCHOLOGICAL PERSPECTIVE
Psychologically, what is striking about this scenario is the experience of separation and exile on unaccompanied minors, and bullying by young people of each other, including those from a different ethnic background.

Without the care of a parent or guardian or extended family, these children lack key psychological sources of security and support. Many have experienced trauma and bereavement, and all have come through separation and undergone loss of some sort (i.e. loss of family, friends, culture or identity). Feelings of fear and insecurity, anxiety about their future and coming to terms with the trauma and events that have led to their arrival in another country make this an extremely emotional and distressing experience for children. Children separated from the security of family, home and country experience feelings of loss and uprootedness. The often hidden nature of their predicament, their tenuous economic state, the difficulties they encounter in trying to establish their entitlement to protection, as well as their lack of knowledge of how to survive in a foreign 'adult' world all exacerbate the stress they experience (Ayotte, 2000).

The Separated Children in Europe Programme has highlighted that unaccompanied minors should be seen and treated as children and individuals first and foremost, rather than simply as migrants subject to administrative and immigration controls. What children like Karim need is to feel safe and help to cope with being separated from their families, homes and cultures. In the field of psychology, Maslow's (1943) theory of a 'hierarchy of needs' has highlighted how 'feeling safe' underpins mental health and well-being. For the children, understanding about their present and future is critical to this. Knowing what is to happen to them is important to alleviate the distress and worry they have about their lives, and Claire and other care staff can help with this. Thus, professionals play a key role in helping children to understand the processes involved in tracing relatives to assist with repatriation, and, for other children, the processes involved in seeking and obtaining asylum. In addition, feeling comfortable and safe where they live is also paramount to enhancing their sense of safety. Separated children should not feel vulnerable or scared where they live. They should feel that they have someone to go to for help whom they can trust, and with whom they can build up a relationship. Often, this might be someone like Claire, or a key-worker in the hostel where they live. A sense of safety and security is also built up by the children having routines and a sense of predictability and consistency in their lives. Knowing the pattern of their day and what can be expected reduces worry about unexpected or unpredictable events and concern over not knowing what is going on in their life.

Attachment theory (proposed by theorists such as Bowlby and Ainsworth) has emphasised the harmful and disturbing impact of the separation from loved ones. Prolonged separation from loved ones can be particularly damaging to a child's emotional well-being and future relationships. Separations which are abrupt are considered to be among the most distressing because children are not prepared for them (Fahlberg, 1991). Grief, a diminished sense of trust, fear of future loss and poor self-esteem are just some of the possible consequences from separation. Some separated children are reunited with their families either in their country of origin or within Ireland. These children need help to prepare for such reunification and in rebuilding their familial relationships. However, as Mooten (2006) noted, support for such children is often overlooked, despite the fact that the separation experience can have a damaging psychological effect on both parent and child. Follow-up care for reunited families has been recommended by Mooten (2006) amongst others. Attachment theory has also drawn attention to the value of nurturing a sense of continuity with what one has lost or been separated from. Claire and other staff could help Karim have contact with people from his own culture. Veale and colleagues (2003) reported that in Dublin there have been good experiences reported where minors were placed in accommodation centres with family groups from their country of origin, with the adults acting as role models, helping the minors.

Secondly, therapeutic work may be needed for any trauma experienced and can help children to work through their feelings of grief and loss. Violence, torture, rape, murder, kidnapping, traumatic bereavement and natural disasters, such as earthquakes and floods, are examples of some of the forms of trauma encountered. These can all be deeply upsetting, contributing to anxiety, behavioural problems, intrusive memories, eating and sleeping disorders, somatic complaints, and a lack of trust in relationships. Sometimes, traumatic experiences can induce regressive behavioural problems, such as enuresis, as well as self-harming behaviour. The HSE Psychological Service for Refugees and Asylum Seekers provides services for children including 'self developmental group work' for separated adolescents. According to Mooten (2006), young people in this programme feel they 'think too much', expressing concerns over separation and loss from their families, the welfare of their families, uncertainty about their asylum claim, an inability to plan their future education or career, racism and daily stressors associated with living in exile and a lack of social support' (Ree in Veale et al., 2003; Trang & Lau, 2002). Individual needs also present which require more specific intervention and support. According to Veale and colleagues (2003, p. 40):

> There are also many separated children with special needs, such as sibling guardians of younger children, pregnant girls, young mothers and their infants, and depressed or withdrawn youth who may not come to the attention of social workers, who have significant guardianship needs.

Thirdly, children can be helped to enhance their coping skills and overall resilience. Resilience has been defined as 'qualities which cushion a vulnerable child from the worst effects of adversity in whatever form it takes and which may help a child or young person to cope, survive and even thrive in the face of great hurt and disadvantage' (Gilligan, 1997, p. 12). In building a child's resilience, consideration should be given to enhancing social supports, such as their friendships, and their relationships with people to whom they can go to for help and guidance. This can involve helping a child to strengthen their friendships and helping professionals, such as key-workers, social workers and teachers, to encourage the child to see them as people to whom they can go to for support. Reflective work is also important to uncover the child's perspective and to help them to understand what has happened to them, what may happen in their future, and to increase their sense of 'self-efficacy' or control in their own life. For example, a child's views on decisions regarding family reunification should be given due weight in accordance with the child's age and maturity (European Commission, 2004). A sense of direction is important for children in difficult circumstances, as it can enhance feelings of stability and control. For example, Claire could help Karim to identify goals in his life and plans for reaching them. A child's interests and hobbies, such as Karim's interest in fishing, are also ways of helping them cope as they provide an 'enjoyable space', a time away from feeling worried and distraught. Hobbies, sports and other interests can also be an avenue through which friendships and relationships can be forged. In the words of Robert, a 16-year-old separated child in Ireland:

> Being an unaccompanied minor is not easy, especially in a strange country all by yourself. At first the process of asylum is complicated for most minors especially because most of the time we are treated as adults when it comes to the asylum process and are expected to produce the same documents relating to our stories as adults would. Most minors understand why evidence and proofs must be provided but feel that the government and asylum system should be a bit easier on us since when we leave our countries, documents are the last thing we think of. When it comes to school most minors are a bit intimidated mainly because the system of education is often different from the school system in our countries of origin. As a result, we feel that we might fall behind, but on the other hand many of us adapt to the system, sometimes even more than others . . . Racism is one of the other intimidating subjects for minors. According to the minors I have spoken to, almost 90 per cent have experienced racism, either directly, or indirectly. Even though these experiences can be quite traumatizing, most of us tend to be optimistic and we don't let racism hold us back, we also think positively about the outcome of the asylum applications.
>
> (Mooten, 2006, p. 57)

In this practice scenario Claire has seen some bullying of the Nigerian teenagers by some Irish teenagers. Bullying has been defined as an imbalance of strength (physical and/or psychological), a deliberate intention to hurt another with little if any provocation and repeated negative actions against another person (Olweus, 1993). It can include name-calling, teasing, being picked on, being hit and pushed around, being made fun of or being left out or 'ostracised'. It can have very serious effects, undermining a child's self-esteem and mental health and contributes to depression, loneliness, self-harm and suicide (Wilkins-Shurmer et al., 2003). Research with Irish adolescents has indicated that one in fifty young people are bullied on a weekly basis, and that the incidence peaks in the second year of secondary school (approximate age 14 years). Verbal bullying (e.g. name-calling, rumour-spreading) was the most common form reported (55 per cent) followed by physical (25 per cent) and psychological bullying including exclusion (14 per cent) (O'Moore, Kirkham & Smith, 1997). This shows that bullying is a worryingly prevalent problem amongst children and young people. Such bullying may at times be construed as racism, a concern voiced by separated children attending the HSE psychological service for Refugees and Asylum Seekers self-developmental group work (Ree in Veale et al., 2003). Whether considered to be racially based or not, bullying does compromise a child's sense of safety and well-being. Consequently, Claire and her colleagues should consider the best way to encourage the children in care to open up and disclose bullying experiences and to help them to identify helpful and unhelpful responses, as well as strategies to deal with it and who to go to for help. Further action may be needed, such as informing the school. Inclusive initiatives involving children and their families in the locality with the separated children might also reduce the incidence of separated children being targets of bullying as they come to be more integrated into peer groups. In addition, involving families might help to reduce any bullying triggered by racist attitudes picked up in the home.

Psychological issues highlighted in this practice scenario include: impact of attachment separation and trauma, prejudice, identity formation and social belonging, and peer acceptance/rejection.

PROFESSIONAL PERSPECTIVE
The context for this discussion on professional practice issues is a Drop-in Youth Project. The focus is on the professional skills and challenges that are associated with cultural diversity. It is important to state at the outset that youth work and social care are distinct professions. Youth Work is defined as 'a planned programme of education designed for the purpose of aiding and enhancing the personal and social development of young persons through their voluntary involvement' (Government of Ireland Youth Work Act 2001). Social care, on the other hand, is described as being 'committed to the planning and delivery of quality care and other support services for individuals with identified needs' (IASCE 2005). Whilst there is a clear distinction in both approach and professional relationship, there are increasing overlaps between these professions. The scenario in focus here allows discussions of practice issues common to both professions.

Cultural diversity is a fact of life in twenty-first century Ireland. In recent years, Ireland has experienced a rapid growth in ethnic, religious and cultural diversity. The Census (Government of Ireland, 2006) shows that one in ten of Ireland's population is now non-Irish. This diversity builds on the diversity that always existed in Ireland (albeit in relatively small numbers) and which includes the Travelling Community, Jewish, Muslim, Asian and African communities. The example under discussion here reflects the reality of the challenge – and opportunities – that result from this diversity. At the official launch of the European Year of Intercultural Dialogue 2008, the European Commissioner for Education, Ján Figel declared:

We want to move beyond multicultural societies, where cultures and cultural groups simply coexist side by side, where we live 'parallel lives'. We need to become intercultural societies where plurality of cultures cooperates in dialogue and in shared responsibility.

We will now look at some of the key skills required in promoting interculturalism.

The Youth Project that provides the setting for this scenario is typical of a targeted response to meeting the needs of young people in defined disadvantaged areas. The 'drop-in' nature of the service is designed to engage young people in activities and provide opportunities for discussion, education and social interactions with peers and leaders. In examining this scenario, three areas of professional practice will be discussed: *engagement*, *planning* and *cultural awareness*. The discussion here is informed by the comments of both professionals in the youth work field and by young people recently settled in Ireland.

Engagement

Professional social care is based on relationships. These relationships often create the space in which meaningful and positive change can occur. Hawkins and Shohet (2002) describe the work of the professional social care worker as protecting this therapeutic space. In the informal context of the drop-in project given in our example, it is essential that opportunities be created in which marginalised young people can begin to overcome the isolation they experience in moving from home to a new and different country and culture.

Professional's comment: 'The challenge for Claire is that the issues described need to be tackled at so many different levels. A starting point might be to devise and facilitate an activity that would be attractive for all the 'drop-in' teenagers. This would give her an opportunity to engage with the boys from different cultures and get a picture of their needs.'

The engagement activity therefore serves two purposes: firstly, to overcome isolation and begin to break down barriers; secondly, to create opportunities that establish professional relationships in order to identify needs and plan future work. The skills associated with this aspect of the work again cluster around the relationship-building task. Communication, both verbal and non-verbal, are essential and need to adapt to the setting – in this scenario the 'organised chaos' of a teenage gathering! Listening skills can sometimes be taken for granted. Claire has shown here a capacity to listen not just to what has been said but to the underlying messages being communicated by the service users that have the potential to alienate one group from another.

Young person's reflection: 'A young Polish woman I spoke to could easily relate to the young people in the example. She saw their starting point as one of isolation, away from their family, their language and the things that are familiar to them. They need the opportunity to meet new people and gain confidence in their new surroundings. Sometimes the opposite happens and other young people reject them.'

Planning

The reality for many people newly arrived in Ireland is that they are located at the edge of the local community, be it physically in the way that they are housed (often together, temporarily and institutionally), socially, by language and cultural difference, and economically, by limited educational and employment opportunities. The first reaction of the professional interviewed about our example was that the response needed to happen at many different levels. The response, therefore, needs to be planned over time, with clear objectives and with some way of measuring its success.

Because of the nature of social care work, outcomes are often open-ended. This is because the ultimate aim is long-term. This, however, does not mean that we should abandon all efforts at evaluating our work. The scenario in question here does indeed have a long-term aim of integrating young people into the indigenous population – something that might only be measured two generations from now! It is possible, though, to measure shorter term outcomes, such as instances of integration, higher levels of cross-cultural communication, improvements in social, educational and economic opportunities, reduction in incidents of racial discrimination and abuse.

The challenges involved in this aspect of the work can prove both demanding and exciting for Claire and her colleagues. The skill-set required to address these challenges is clustered around what could be described as 'empowerment social care work' (Miley et al., 2004). This concept places the role of the professional worker as *working with* rather than *working for* vulnerable people or groups. It sees advocacy and enabling skills as integral to the social care worker's job. This in turn demands of the worker an understanding of not just the effects of societal injustice but also an ability to work towards challenging their causes. Good research and writing skills are necessary. Claire has shown a capacity to reflect and a willingness to work as part of a wider team in planning a response to the immediate and longer term needs of the young people she observed in the course of her work.

Cultural Awareness

It was clear from talking with a young person who recently arrived in Ireland that the immediate challenges Karim faced were as much to do with being away from family and friends as specifically the result of being culturally different. However, these feelings of loneliness and isolation were more severe because of cultural differences and a further barrier was created by Karim's not speaking English fluently. Indeed it was the ability to identify these barriers and to focus on ways to overcome them that marked the professional interviewed as being culturally sensitive. She recommended English language classes as being important in building confidence. When asked to comment further on the scenario above, her focus centred on 'a big activity towards team-building'. The experienced professional explained that the aim here is to begin to break down barriers. A shared positive experience that enables all the young people who use the service to participate equally can create opportunities to explore cultural difference together.

The cultural competence (i.e. the set of relevant skills) displayed by the professional here is based on an understanding of interculturalism. It reflects the five themes that form the basis of an intercultural framework set out in The National Action Plan Against Racism (Department of Justice, Equality & Law Reform, 2008), Protection, Inclusion, Provision, Recognition and Participation. These themes point towards direct action and place an onus on the worker to ensure that the agency is responding to its service-users on a number of levels. In our scenario, Claire has used observation and recording skills in responding to her initial concern for the welfare of the young non-Irish boys using the drop-in service. She is aware that she is not alone in her professional role and sets about bringing the team together to discuss an action plan. Teamwork skills are key here; indeed, the promotion of inclusion of non-Irish young people into the general activities of the project challenges the team as a whole to assess its own readiness for this new work.

Creative work was identified in the professional interview as an approach to overcoming barriers that exist amongst diverse groups. The worker must have an openness and willingness to organise creative activities. The value of such activities, such as arts and crafts, group games and cookery, was verified by the young Polish woman when asked what aspect of the youth service that she used helped most. She went on to explain that these activities helped to break down the language barriers but also the social barriers. One of the biggest obstacles for a new arrival is to make meaningful contact with peers from the host community. In fact, for this young person and for the young people in our example, their first experience of their Irish peers was negative, as they were excluded from the group and even more directly by racist comments. The role of creative work in this context is more than merely bringing people together: it is to establish opportunities for the young service-users to meet and engage with one another in an environment that is non-threatening and mutually respectful. In planning creative activities, the worker must be aware of their multi-functional properties.

Skills Grid

	Engagement	Planning	Cultural Awareness
Familiar	Relationship-building	Writing/Research	Self-awareness
	Communication	Reflection	Creativity
	Listening	Teamwork	Group work
	Group facilitation		

	Engagement	Planning	Cultural Awareness
Unfamiliar	Cultural awareness	Multi-level planning	Identity self-awareness
	Welcoming skills	Negotiation	Foreign language

Professional practice issues highlighted in this practice scenario include: life-space intervention, intercultural work and enhancing resilience.

Minority populations need to be able to maintain their ethnic identities even while seeking inclusion in the societal mainstream (Lum, 2004). Lum goes on to identify the factors that form ethnic identity as, 'skin colour, name, language, common religious beliefs, common ancestry, and place of origin'. The worker needs to be aware of their own role in creating positive spaces in which minority and majority groups can explore their own and each others' identities. The skills identified and discussed in this section are not exhaustive, but are informed by the comments and insights of a service-provider with hands-on experience of working with young people from different ethnic backgrounds and by a young person recently arrived in Ireland. As the profession of social care evolves, professionals and students need to identify, critique, adopt and adapt a range of skills that serves the specific purposes of social care. The skills grid summarises those in use in the above example. The grid also includes some less familiar skills that are also applicable.

– 2 –

Access and Empowerment

- Impairment is defined as 'an injury, illness, or congenital condition that causes or is likely to cause a long-term effect on physical appearance and/or limitation of function within the individual that differs from the commonplace' (Combat Poverty Agency, 2005).
- Disability is defined as 'the loss or limitation of opportunities to take part in society on an equal level with others due to social and environmental barriers' (ibid.).
- With a developing understanding of disability in Ireland, there are presently 25,613 people registered on the National Intellectual Disability Database (2008) equating to 6 per 1,000 members in the population, an increase of 31 per cent since 1974.
- Of the registered population of intellectually disabled, 97 per cent currently avail of either residential or day services, showing 64 per cent living with a family member and a 66 per cent reduction of individuals living in psychiatric hospitals since 1966 (ibid.).
- Individuals who experience a persistent disability are 42 per cent less likely to be employed than individuals without persistent disabilities (Gannon and Nolan, 2006).
- Individuals with a long-term or chronic disability have a 9 per cent reduction in levels of social participation (ibid.), measured in terms of regular participation in a club, neighbourhood activity, political party, etc.

Practice Scenario 2

Setting - Community Residence

Fintan has a moderate intellectual disability, and at 19 years of age has just moved out of his family home and into a house in the community with three other service-users because his parents have been ill recently and felt that it was better for him to move into sheltered housing. Fintan has settled well into the house and enjoys the company of the people living and working there. He loves going bowling with the others in the house every Thursday evening, and especially looks forward to their stop at the local chipper on the way home.

As a part of the service provided to Fintan, there is an opportunity to attend a training workshop working in a large retail shop once per week. Fintan is eager to participate and could take a bus from near the house directly to the workshop and back. Going to the training workshop would make Fintan feel like the rest of his housemates because each of the others work in different places one or two days per week.

In addition to the lads in the house, Fintan spends time with his older cousin Jim and admires him a lot as he is good at football and seems popular amongst his friends. Fintan enjoys watching Jim play at matches and would love to be able to play on a football team. Fintan also gets on well with Jim's girlfriend, Caoimhe, and would love to have a girlfriend like her because she seems so nice and fun to be around. Fintan only knows a few girls from the school he goes to and is hoping that he will meet more at the large retail unit when he goes on training.

Hearing of Fintan's new training opportunity, his parents are reluctant and anxious about him working in such a mainstream setting because they fear it will not protect him from ill-intentioned people. They are already concerned about the fact that since he moved out of home he has tried smoking and drinks beer when he goes on trips. They are also concerned that Fintan has mentioned that he is going to find a girlfriend after he starts working. Fintan wishes his parents didn't fuss and worry so much about him.

For further consideration...

- What further decisions and/or actions should be taken by professional care workers when considering Fintan's health and well-being, safety and social inclusion?
- In what ways can a social care practitioner use their professional skills and knowledge to facilitate the following for Fintan?
  - Inclusion/participation
  - Equality and social status
  - Decision-making power/agency
- How can Fintan's development, as an adult, be best facilitated?
- How can we assess a person's level of informed understanding about the risks and benefits of the choices they make? (The difficulty in care-work is 'walking the line' between caring and protecting service-users while empowering them to be more independent and to take risks in the choices they make.)
- Look again at the scenario and identify the elements of Fintan's situation associated with each of the empowerment skills in the grid that follows the Professional Perspective.

SOCIOLOGICAL PERSPECTIVE

Disabilities have more recently been analysed through a social as well as a medical lens. This change has introduced a view held by many that physical and mental impairments have been socially constructed. Labels are attached to individuals that accept – and expect – restricted activity, thereby calling them 'disabled'. Social issues such as oppression, difference and various 'isms' are common themes in the emerging discourse of disability. Taking a materialist perspective, Oliver (1990, 1996), Barnes (1996, 1998) and Thomas (1999, 2001, 2002) have independently argued that with the increase of large-scale industry, people with impairments began to be excluded from employment and economic activity because they were perceived as less able to join the paid workforce under the demanding and standardised intensity of factory work. This exclusion from the labour force in the nineteenth and twentieth centuries was labelled as a 'social problem', and people with impairments increasingly experienced barriers in employment as well as in social services. While an individual may have an impairment resulting from a biological, physical or mental condition, their relationship with society reflects the values and labels created and sustained by social regulations and agreed norms. Individuals with impairments are often categorised into groups based on an identified 'difference', becoming socially arranged and marginalised. (For a feminist view of this distinction see Shildrick & Price, 1996; Corker, 1998; Corker & French, 1999.)

In the scenario above, Fintan has successfully engaged with other service-users and family members, demonstrating that he has the abilities as an individual to make contributions to a community home setting. He has begun to show that he has the competencies required for independent living, and he wishes to expand his opportunities. Fintan has observed and participated in a variety of activities, and now has clearly identified and expressed his needs and short-term goals. Although Fintan's impairment is moderate, his well-intentioned parents and society at large view it as a disability that has social restrictions and one that may create social problems. If Fintan's life experiences are shaped by his disability, he will continue to be excluded from the social environment that others take for granted. Baker and colleagues (2004) suggest that this exclusion will mark him as different, even strange, reinforcing a stereotype that may promote isolation and discourage relationships of love, care and solidarity with others.

In addition to an economic explanation of disability and marginalisation, there are alternative perspectives for social care workers to consider. A sociological perspective sees social values as reflecting cultural concepts of access, power and agreed policies. These help to explain society's view of citizenship and equality. Citizenship not only signifies equality between citizens, but equality in the way that the state relates to its citizens. In Western Europe, the state is not only obliged to meet the basic needs of its citizens but also to facilitate meaningful participation in society. (For further discussion on this see Jensen & Phillips, 1996; Kymlinka & Norman, 1995; Marshall, 1963; Roeher, 1993 and Rioux, 2003). In the past, the majority of social policies enabled professional control (i.e. institutionalisation) more than the independence and participation of individuals with impairments. Fintan has expressed his personal wish to participate in mainstream employment, to socialise with his peers (both male and female), and to occasionally enjoy a drink and cigarette when he goes out. It is questionable, however, whether his rights to fully participate in society are compromised at present or whether social care workers should intervene to facilitate his social participation. When the conditions of full membership of and inclusion in society are limited for individuals with impairments, citizenship is diminished. Look objectively at the restrictions being considered for him regarding mainstream work and socialising; the very essence of Fintan's social equality and status may be reduced by such restrictions. Social care practice is grounded in a commitment to increase the influence that a service-user has in his or her life and to empower their level of social, economic and political participation. Working with Fintan, a care worker's objective would be to advocate and facilitate his access and inclusion to the same standard typically available to his non-impaired counterparts.

Sociological issues highlighted in this practice scenario include: discrimination based on disability, inclusion/participation, decision-making and agency, access and power, welfare systems and policies, citizenship and civil rights, social status and equality.

PSYCHOLOGICAL PERSPECTIVE
From a psychological perspective, this scenario highlights the roles of choice and independence, which are key components of facilitating empowerment and enabling access to opportunities in life. The importance of independence, choice and personal fulfilment are advocated strongly in humanistic psychology. In reaction to both behaviourist psychology and psychoanalytic psychology, the humanistic school of psychology emerged in the 1950s. It has its roots in existentialist philosophy and emphasises the positive aspects of human nature, individuality and personal strengths, as opposed to human weaknesses, problems or 'pathology'.

Carl Rogers is one of the most famous humanistic psychologists. Rogers highlighted the importance of people 'realizing their potential', honesty or 'authenticity' and a 'non-judgmental' stance in relationships (discussed later in Practice Scenario Nine). He also emphasised the importance of recognising that each person experiences the world in a unique, individual way. Thus, we can never assume how another person sees, feels, thinks or experiences events. To help people feel 'psychologically safe', Rogers emphasised the role of 'unconditional positive regard', whereby respect and regard is accorded to a person notwithstanding their problems, disabilities or behaviour. Applying these ideas to the scenario, it is good that Fintan is being supported in living in sheltered housing, which gives him more independence and integration in the community. Fintan should be facilitated to do what he wants to do, realise his potential and maximise his abilities. Attending the training workshop would be a positive initiative for Fintan, as it would give him the opportunity to work like the others in the house and to be more a part of the community in which he lives. This would mean that he would feel more like his housemates, and not 'the odd one out' of the group. Furthermore, it would provide him with more experiences to talk about with his housemates and colleagues and would likely enhance his self-esteem and confidence. Playing football with a team would also enhance Fintan's self-esteem and happiness as this is something he is interested in and wants to do. Football is a healthy, sociable and fun activity which might bring more happiness, personal enjoyment and a wider range of friends into Fintan's life.

Martin Seligman developed some of Rogers' ideas further, focusing particularly on happiness and well-being. According to Seligman (2002), happiness consists of three components:

- **A pleasant life**: experiencing positive emotions about the present, past and future (satisfaction from doing things that are enjoyable, feelings of contentment and fulfilment from having done things enjoyed in the past, feelings of hope, trust and optimism in looking to the future).
- **An engaged life**: being involved and absorbed in activities, such as relationships, work and leisure pursuits; engaging in talents and interests; becoming 'lost' in things.
- **A meaningful life**: using strengths and talents towards something important and meaningful; working, spending time with others, pursuing objectives which are personally valued.

Having a girlfriend and a close, possibly intimate, relationship is also something that may make Fintan happier. This should be covered in Fintan's person-centred planning, and related opportunities should be sought which might help Fintan build friendships and relationships with the opposite sex. Attention needs to be paid to what Fintan understands, expects and desires from such a relationship. Serious consideration also would need to be given to health and safety issues, risks and possible outcomes as well as preparation for how Fintan would cope with the specific problems posed by such a relationship, and what supports could be put in place.

Providing Fintan with more independence and choice means letting him make the choices he wants, even if others, such as care staff and family, disagree. When it is felt that his choices don't put his welfare at risk and that he can make an informed choice, being aware of the consequences of such a choice (both good and bad), the matter should rest with Fintan. But what is serious risk? Some might say that smoking and drinking are risky choices, yet adults often choose to do these.

O'Brien (1989) and O'Brien and O'Brien (1998) identified five valued experiences which contribute to a meaningful life and which can be usefully applied within person-centred planning in care work with people with disabilities. They are: sharing ordinary places, growing in relationships, making choices, contributing and being respected. These can be seen to apply to this scenario as Fintan, through work and leisure, is sharing 'ordinary places' with others. He is building relationships with his housemates and wants to build relationships with the opposite sex. He has been making choices, even though some of these, such as his smoking and drinking, are not condoned by his parents. He now contributes more in terms of his work and recreation and through these, his relationships and his likely involvement in his own person-centred planning, he probably feels more respected. The five valued experiences according to O'Brien (1989) encompass eight primary areas which can also be seen as indicators of quality in care provision. These are:

1. Care planning and care practices which articulate the individual's vision for a desirable future and individualised responses to that vision.
2. People who know and who care about the individual are included in the design of the plan and subsequent services. People who can assist the person in moving forward toward the goal(s) are included in the planning processes.
3. The person is the lead in making life-defining choices related to where to live and work and in relationships. The person is provided with experiences from which to make informed and educated decisions. Opportunities for making decisions are a part of the daily routine.
4. Naturally occurring and common community resources are used where possible (e.g. the person joins day trips to the seaside or attends yoga classes in the community rather than a special group being set up for people with disabilities).
5. A person's interests and talents are taken into account in the context of supportive community environments that facilitate association with

people who share similar interests, capacities and talents.

6. Existing resources are used in novel ways to support the person's interests, capacities and needs, and the person is given as much control as possible over resources.

7. Planning is an ongoing and progressive process. The person has a team of support comprised of individuals who are interested in helping the person to reach their goals.

8. The person expresses satisfaction with his or her relationships, residential and working life, and daily routines. The person can clearly identify his or her goals and express satisfaction with the rate of progress being made towards the realisation of those goals.

Psychological issues highlighted in this practice scenario include: personal development, special needs, Maslow's hierarchy of needs, sexuality and well-being.

PROFESSIONAL PERSPECTIVE

When discussing this scenario with a group of service-users with intellectual disabilities, one word kept coming up: *independence* – independence from home, financial independence, independence to make decisions, and independence to form friendships and relationships. These service-users could clearly identify with Fintan in his desire to have control over how he lives his life. Empowerment is said to be 'about people working to gain control of their lives and to maximise their quality of life, and doing so through self-help strategies' (Ramcharan et al., 2000, p. xi). An emphasis on 'self-help' raises particular questions about the approach and role of the social care worker. Working with a person with disabilities involves enabling the person to identify and achieve their own goals, and requires an approach of 'doing with' rather than 'doing for'. This section will look at the implications of adopting an empowerment stance as a social care professional.

In our scenario, Fintan has reached an important stage in his life. The excitement of moving out of home may be tempered by concern about his parent's health. His focus, however, is on practical issues: getting a job; forming relationships; socialising; settling in to his new surroundings. Whilst it appears that Fintan is capable of achieving autonomy or independence in all of these areas, his moderate intellectual disability means that he will require support in negotiating a pathway towards and maintaining independence in some or all of these areas. It is the task of the social care worker to provide appropriate levels of support to allow Fintan to 'gain power of decision and action over his own life' (Payne, 1997, p. 266). This may be achieved through 'reducing the effect of social or personal blocks to exercising power and by transforming power from the environment to [Fintan]' (ibid.).

Supporting a person with a disability requires the social care worker to use a range of skills and to have an understanding of the context in which the person is living. Finnerty and Collins (2005, p. 278) put it clearly by saying:

> When a person has a disability, quality of life depends on a number of factors:
> - The nature of the disability
> - The person's adaptations to their disability
> - The level of support from the immediate family
> - How society views and responds to the disability.

When discussing Fintan's scenario with two professional social care workers (in this instance their job title was Rehabilitative Training Instructor), they emphasised this holistic approach to support. They described the 'Skills for Life' programme at their centre as one that promoted independence while recognising the obstacles that wider society often places in the paths of people with disabilities achieving their potential. The social model of disability service provision locates the cause of disability not in the person who experiences the impairment, but in society's response (Finnerty & Collins, 2005). The workers went on to identify the support of and communication with the families of service-users as a key element of their work. They pointed to the diverse range of reaction, acceptance, attitude and understanding of parents and family to the child's disability. The importance of the professional social care worker's awareness of differing family response needs to be stressed. 'If we are to work in a respectful partnership with parents we have to accept the reality of their interpretations and not oppose or ignore them' (Cunningham & Davis, 1985, cited in Dale, 1997, p. 61).

Empowerment Skills

Much has been written on empowerment and its importance as a central component of social care and social work. But what is the skill-set needed to ensure that the professional is promoting an empowerment approach? Our discussion so far has identified that the worker needs to be able to pay attention to the individual needs, plans and dreams of each service-user. This demands heightened communication and listening skills as well as an ability to plan and evaluate actions. An understanding of family and societal attitudes towards disability is also a key requirement; this in turn leads to the need to develop negotiation skills. The service-users we spoke to stressed the practical skills gained at their training centre as being most useful. This indicates that the social care worker may need to be able to motivate, support, advise and inform service-users as they make decisions about their future. It is interesting to note that in relation to skills training, the workers at the agency pointed to what they called 'over-certification' by the education and training system for people with disabilities in Ireland of training-centre activities. This led to unrealistic expectations on the part of service-users. These comments by the social care workers at the agency show their ability to critique their own service provision. Critical observation of service provision could therefore be added to the skill-set.

A useful summary of the key elements of empowerment social care work is set out below.

Characteristics of empowerment-centred work*	Competency, or an ability to:
Focus on context	Assess blocks and opportunities presented by contexts, such as family, culture, society at large.
Affirmation of collaboration	Develop a partnership approach with service-users that enables them to take an active part in decision-making.
Emphasis on strengths and opportunities	Work creatively and realistically towards goals with an emphasis on what is possible.
Integration of practice activities at multiple system levels	Respond to challenges and achieving goals may require identifying where changes are needed and not just meeting the immediate needs.
Incorporation of political approach	Promote change action at local, national and international level; take an 'empowerment approach'. Advocacy skills form part of this response.
Commitment to reflection	Engage in both reflection in action and reflection on action is a key skill to ensure effective and appropriate service delivery.

* Based on Miley et al., 2004

Professional issues highlighted in this practice scenario include: empowerment, holistic approach, negotiation skills, motivation skills and self-reflection.

Promoting Independent Living

- By 2011 it is estimated that persons aged 65 and over will represent 14.1 per cent of the Republic's population (Age Action Ireland, 2007).
- By 2050 the number of people over aged 65 will be 29 per cent (Government Publications, 2007).
- The percentage of people over the aged of 65 in 2002 was 11.13 per cent, out of a population of 3,917,203. (Government Publications, 2007).
- In addition to a growing elder population, many older people are living alone. In 2002, 25.8 per cent of older people lived alone (Government Publications, 2007) and this number continues to increase.
- Of the population over the age of 70, which now stands at 266,222, over 33 per cent live alone (Government Publications, 2007).
- Depending on an individual's independence, health and well-being, living alone can easily mean spending from 10-14 hours of one's waking day isolated and excluded from others in the family and/or community (Garavan et al., 2001).

Practice Scenario 3

Setting: Residential Centre for Older People

Nora is 78 and lives alone in a semi-detached house in a city suburb. Despite living in the countryside for over 50 years, Nora agreed with her family to move house after the death of her husband two years ago. Her new neighbours are mainly young couples or young people sharing houses, none of whom she knows, except for the occasional 'hello'. Sometimes Nora feels she is living in an empty estate, especially from 9 a.m. to 5 p.m. on weekdays.

All of Nora's family is scattered: her eldest daughter Catherine is in America, her son Niall is in Dublin with his family and her youngest child Sara is in Australia. Nora talks to her daughters over the phone regularly, especially Catherine who phones each Sunday evening. Niall and his family live about four hours away but they visit every two or three months. Nora loves seeing her two grandchildren, Jaime and Tom, though she feels she doesn't know them well.

Nora's three children bought her a computer last Christmas and Niall continually tries to convince her to use it to keep in touch with the family. Nora is living on a small widow's pension and using the computer to talk with her children and grandchildren would help avoid costly phone bills. Nora doesn't feel confident around new technology and, besides, it's not the same as a phone call with a 'real voice' at the end of the line. She experiences insecurity and is disillusioned with modern technology.

Nora used to work part-time in a post-office in a small village before she retired and she still misses the sense of belonging and contribution the job brought to her life. She has found retirement particularly difficult since her husband died. Nora often thinks back to the years when she would meet everyone from the village on a daily basis at Mass, the local shops and regular coffee mornings. Her sense of social belonging and participation has greatly changed since moving away from her country home and she feels a loss of worth and sense of belonging.

Now Nora feels lonely and fills much of her time watching television. Her children have encouraged her to do a night class but she's reluctant to join something where she knows no one. She always did want to do ballroom dancing but now she has arthritis, and has had a few risky falls so she thinks that it's better not to try the dancing at this time in her life. She always meant to join the Irish Country Woman's Association but now feels it is too late. Despite her feelings of isolation and loneliness, Nora likes being close to the shops and church, although she only goes out during the day because she is intimidated by some of the local youth who hang about on the corner after dark. Nora has been hurt in the past by their sneers and references to her as 'aul' one' or 'old granny'.

One thing Nora is especially happy to continue is visits with her close friend Paula, who lives in a nearby nursing home. Paula has multiple sclerosis and is unable to move well without assistance. Even with her fixed income, Nora enjoys taking Paula out to get her hair done or to a cafe or the shops. Both women enjoy these outings and Paula prefers them to the regular hairdresser that visits the nursing home. Unfortunately, Nora and Paula can only go out together when there is a nurse's aide free to go with them. Following each visit, Nora tells herself that she would hate to live in a nursing home because she values her independence and personal space. Recognition of Paula's dependence and realisation that this could be her future as well is troublesome for Nora.

For further consideration...

- What are some practical steps that can be implemented to increase social inclusion in Nora's case?
- What social policies and legislation should be considered when consulting an older person about their life choices?
- What intervention can a care practitioner implement to minimise feelings of isolation and loss for an older person?

SOCIOLOGICAL PERSPECTIVE

Due to a variety of developmental factors, societies around the world are experiencing increased life expectancy and a subsequent rise in the ageing population. This has sparked an interest and evaluation of current economic, social and political policies relevant to retirement, pension entitlements, health care, family responsibilities and more. Older people who were formally referred to as enjoying their 'golden years' are now categorised as ending their economic contribution to society and are perceived by some as being economic liabilities.

While challenging the definition of a 'developed' society, sociologists have largely agreed that since the Industrial Revolution, members of society who are economically viable are also more likely to gain access to social participation and services. In a global community now centred on economic production, older people are finding themselves increasingly disenfranchised due to their lack of economic participation, either by choice or forced retirement. Others find that they are unable (or perceived as being unable) to keep up with a demanding and fast-paced life. Economic production, however, that is defined narrowly by involvement in the public sphere of work has been largely criticised by research that challenges the view that paid work (i.e. a wage associated with a day's work) is the only economic contribution to society. Feminist research is well established as identifying the unpaid work in the home and in the community as facilitating other family members to leave the private sphere (i.e. the home) and enter the public sphere of paid work. Sociologists agree that, traditionally, the unpaid work has been carried out by women (e.g. caring for dependent family members, housework, support work) but Lynch (1989) and Lynch and McLaughlin (1995) extend this view by identifying the emotional work is 'love labour' that many people experience on a regular basis. Lynch and McLaughlin challenge social and economic evaluations that have not taken this work into account when assessing the cost of a healthy society.

While most would agree that emotional care and love are essential, society has failed to factor it into our social costs and equations, leaving it largely to the 'natural' and 'innate' responsibility of women, many of whom are working in full-time and part-time paid employment, maintaining primary responsibility for the nurturing and caring of dependent (and other) family members and managing the majority of household duties. Many might argue that we regard and appreciate the emotional and practical contributions made by friends and family and that these are not, in fact, valued less than economic work. However, if this is true, why does Western society rank social status and collective power on the basis of wealth, prosperity and ownership? Poor, aged and dependent individuals do not find themselves in influential spheres, populating the upper echelons of socio-economic management, nor do they benefit from most socio-economic policy decisions.

If we agree that economic production includes paid as well as unpaid contributions, then logic would follow that most members of society would be credited with a form of social currency, offering them full and meaningful participation in society. Unfortunately, the old, infirm and poor are recognised with very little in society's 'accounting system'. Is it simply an oversight on society's part that care and love labour are poorly compensated? A review of the social care profession shows us that care was historically provided by family and friends, voluntary groups and organisations. For a variety of social, political and economic reasons, this provision of care has increasingly moved from the private to the public domain with social care practitioners not only employed in all areas of social life, but more recently requiring academic and professional qualifications.

Even with this significant paradigm shift in caring for society's dependent and vulnerable members, some older members of society remain infirm, isolated, weary or disillusioned. Like Paula in the above scenario, access to care may be a commodity that is purchased (i.e. an elder care facility) or may be facilitated through the goodwill and availability of family members and/or friends such as Nora. Nora continues to make useful, non-economic contributions of care, companionship and love to others, which go largely unnoticed by all except Paula. How can one put a price on such companionship? Because it is so difficult to value love labour in economic terms, should recognition be made in a capitalist society? When largely governed by local, national and even a global economy, emotional work and love labour is often only given a token gesture of appreciation by all except the benefactor – who may in exchange also return love and care.

Despite her contribution of care to Paula, Nora suffers from a sense of loss and insecurity as she faces a deficit in her 'social bank account'. Retired and following the loss of her life partner and husband, Nora is now living in a new area without the support of family and friends. With most people in her neighbourhood away all day at work, Nora is lonely, reminiscing of days when she met people in the village on a daily basis. Nora longs for solidarity with her extended family, friends and a local community, but her recent move has uprooted her well-established links and relationships. This scenario raises a number of issues centred on older people's freedom to make decisions regarding their access and participation in society. A sociological view considers the manner in which Nora's relationships are organised, the way in which she is free to participate with other individuals, groups and structures in society. Nora is living alone and socially placed within physical, economic and social boundaries that minimise or prohibit her opportunities to interact in modern society.

Qualified social care workers are trained to enable elderly service-users to identify their needs and to participate in decisions related to their daily lives and personal goals. While most individuals would hope for their later years to allow independent living, social participation and a flexible lifestyle, some, like Nora's friend Paula, are incapacitated or restricted due to illness. When an individual loses the ability to have control over their life and decisions, principles of social stratification suggest that an inequality of power emerges. This diffused power might be seen in personal, family, political or economic spheres. Nora experiences the frustration of being dependent upon staff in the nursing home for a social outing with her friend Paula. Nora also recognises and fears that this could be her future. Lustbader's research (1995) refers to this dilemma when he describes the possibility of meaningful dependency that might include logical thinking, intimacy with family members and for many a spiritual revival. When individuals find themselves physically dependent, therefore, Lustbader's research endorses social care tenets that maintain successful and meaningful ageing is achievable.

Inequality

Nora might not be considered physically dependent at present, however, she is experiencing a form of social stratification as she goes through her days subjected to socially produced assumptions about old age. Family and casual acquaintances sometimes become uncomfortable with older family members around them and may ignore the relationship. Bytheway (1995) argues that older people are pushed to the margins of society as a result of our attempt to be certain about the changes that come with age, and our efforts to distance ourselves from those who look or act differently (e.g. wrinkled, grey-haired, forgetful, slow or unable to adapt to technology). This distancing can happen as emotional detachment occurs with older family members but it also happens at a societal level. Social inequality is a result of relationship inequality, that is, relationships involving individuals, groups and social structures. When wealth, power and privileges are distributed unequally at different stages of life, older members of society become disadvantaged. Having less access to resources, older members of society become less powerful, less recognised and less respected. (For a wider discussion on equality, see Baker et al., 2004). In the scenario with Nora and Paula, this inequality appears unacceptable at every level; however, it continues to prevail and is even defended by our social agreement to endorse values, practices and policies that camouflage inequality and disadvantage.

Social values (i.e. what society deems to be good or bad, right or wrong) are constructed in such a way as to disadvantage the aged. One example of socially structured disadvantage in older people's lives is their forced dependency or disadvantage as a result of mandatory retirement. Nora's part-time work in the post-office provided her with independent income, while at the same time offering her a social network and sense of contribution. With retirement and the loss of her husband, Nora's 'place' in society became economically as well as socially compromised.

Ageism

Ageism refers to the practice of treating people differently exclusively on the grounds of age due to perceived differences related to the ageing process. The concept of ageism was first introduced during the 1960s through the work of Robert Butler (1975), who explored conditions affecting older people in America and, as a result, made recommendations that included changes at political, cultural, personal and psychological levels. Like stratification, ageism is associated with social values and behaviour that discriminate against older people. The National Council on Aging and Older People (2004) claims that a sizable number of elderly are placed in institutional care for social reasons rather than physical or mental reasons. It is when views such as these form the basis of decisions and practices in our society that prejudice and discrimination against the elderly justifies social disadvantages and marginalisation for older people (see also O'Shea, 2003).

While sociologists have identified situations in societies where ageism is prevalent, social care practitioners are in an influential place to effect change. Concerns of dignity and respect are central to their delivery of care, despite low levels of state funding and policy that facilitate social engagement, independent living and community participation. Pierce (2008) identifies the 'enormous problem' of age-related care dominating social policy across Europe from the 1940s onwards and Walker (1999) highlights the changes in retirement and labour market policies that instituted the reconstruction of ageing (i.e. leaving the labour market at age 65, thereby entering 'old age'). Old age became a social 'crisis' and was seen as a liability for economic growth, health and social services. In contrast, a model of positive ageing has taken the forefront with the realisation that many older people possess valuable knowledge, experiences, and skills that contribute to a balanced and inclusive society. Quinn (1999) challenges us to defy the power of ageism by facing the reality that it is a shared experience and to see ourselves in terms of the broader context of the whole of our lives.

Sociological issues highlighted in this practice scenario include: isolation, marginalisation, power relationships, management, decision-making, participation, insecurity/disillusionment with technology, medical concerns and fears of social/physical dependence, and equality.

PSYCHOLOGICAL PERSPECTIVE
Psychologically, what is striking about this scenario is firstly, the experience of bereavement and loss; secondly, the experience of loneliness and ill-health on well-being; and thirdly, the significance of independence for well-being.

Old Age: it's all in the mind?
For the psychologist Erik Erikson (1986), old age or 'later life' involves the stage of 'integrity vs. despair'. This is where a person attempts to strive to experience a sense of wholeness or integrity and acceptance of their life and the choices they made. Feelings of regret, missed opportunities, wasted time or failure to realise goals can undermine a person's self-acceptance and comfort in their life, contributing to despair, poor well-being and a fear of the end of life.

People's definition of 'old age' tends to be closely related to their own age, and is almost never below it. For this reason, women tend to see old age as starting later than men. In general, most old people do not consider themselves as old, and 70 years is generally selected as the minimum age for the onset of old age (Daly & O'Connor, 1984, p. 48).

From the older person's perspective, chronological age does not necessarily relate to '*felt age*'. It is a general feeling that a positive attitude to life and mixing in the community contributes to keeping a person 'young and active'. Chronological age is nevertheless widely used to categorise people, paradoxically, even by the older people themselves (Daly & O'Connor, 1984, p. 49). In the words of older people:

> I think if you moan and groan all the time it does not help. It makes you look old and feel old. I think a cheerful outlook on life is best.

> It's your attitude to life. You are as young as you feel. Going out and meeting people is a great help. If you sit back and say that you have become too old to go out that is the end.
> (Daly & O'Connor, 1984, p. 48)

Many older people, like Nora, overcome difficulties, such as physical isolation, ill health and lack of transport, to maintain a hopeful and contented perspective on their lives. Others, however, are despondent and negative in their attitudes, being pessimistic about their future and feeling little cared for and much neglected. It is not that their circumstances are very much worse than those of the former group, but it is their attitudes to these circumstances that differ (ibid.).

What are the factors that affect the process of ageing? Irish research with older people highlights the role of worries or troubles; a person's attitude and reaction to ageing and to life events and finally, health and care for one's self as factors influencing the process of ageing (Daly & O'Connor, 1984). Two main positive features of ageing were identified by older people: financial and other forms of provision for older people made by the state, and the fact that one can take it easy because one's formal working life is over (ibid.).

According to Rowe and Kahn (1987), successful ageing is characterised by active involvement in life and living, high cognitive and physical functioning and being free of disability and disease. Active ageing is a process of optimising opportunities for physical, mental and social well-being throughout life in order to extend healthy life expectancy, quality of life and productivity in older age. The term 'active ageing' is now commonly used to describe continuing involvement in social, cultural, spiritual and economic areas (Coakley, 2003). Capacity-building for voluntary and active retirement groups at community level is also necessary for the fulfilment of healthy ageing goals. The Healthy Ageing Programme can play a major role in this regard by acting as a valuable resource to support voluntary groups in achieving best practice in the operation of healthy ageing projects (O'Shea & Connolly, 2003).

Bereavement

Not only did Nora lose her husband two years ago, and may still be grieving over him, but she has also lost the social circle of her husband's friends that she interacted with. As a consequence of moving from the countryside to a city suburb, Nora has also 'lost' her past neighbours. Since her retirement, she has also lost the occupational role she used have as a post-office worker. Furthermore, she has 'lost' her children in terms of physical proximity as they now all live far away from her.

In attempting to understand how people deal with loss, several models of bereavement and grief have been developed. These include stage and process models of grief, which include reactions ranging across the spectrum of 'active distress', such as anger, to 'passive despair', such as apathy and withdrawal. Many highlight initial feelings of disbelief, shock and numbness followed by feelings of anger, yearning and sadness and disorientation. Numbness and disbelief correspond to the Freudian defence mechanisms of denial, repression and dissociation. Habitual actions, like setting a place for someone no longer there, may persist. Intrusive thoughts about the loss and its implications are other features of grief. Such obsessional thinking about the bereaved person is also often associated with negative emotions about the loss. Kubler-Ross (1973) identified typical grief reactions as:

Denial
Failure to recognise or acknowledge the loss. Preoccupation with thoughts of the deceased is considered a feature of 'intrusive thought processes'. Preoccupation is often linked with the need to relive times shared and to go over the events of the loss, more especially if these were distressing or unexpected.

Anger
Annoyance, hostility and fury with the person for dying and with others for being alive. 'If-only' thoughts or 'counterfactuals' refer to when a grieving person ruminates over past events, considering the possibility of alternative scenarios. Anger is typically involved in any separation distress and can be regarded as a basic emotional response to loss (Archer, 1999). Its form and intensity will depend on how the loss is rationalised and attributed, or 'explained' by the individual in making sense of the loss.

Bargaining
Trying to negotiate a deal with God for someone to stay alive.

Depression
Feelings of sorrow, apathy, helplessness and hopelessness. Depression can be 'reactive' in terms of being a reaction to loss, or 'preparatory', in which a person mourns, in advance, the loss of different aspects of their life or the future loss of others. In the word of March and Doherty (2001, p. 495):

> Elderly people who have lived a full life have relatively little to mourn. They have gained much and have lost few opportunities and so they may suffer little preparatory depression. On the other hand, people who review their life and perceive a life of mistakes and missed opportunities may paradoxically have more to mourn as they begin to realize that these opportunities are now lost forever.

Acceptance
The calm acknowledgement of, and adaptation to, the loss. A conscious decision to accept it, that 'life goes on' may often be evident. Such phases

and the order of these are not definitive. While grieving is ultimately a very individual experience, social support is known to play a significant role in how well people adapt to loss.

Many theorists see grief as more appropriately described as a *process* rather than a series of stages through which a person proceeds. According to Fahlberg (1991, p. 41): 'Grief is the process through which one passes in order to recover from a loss.' Viewing grief as a process allows for greater flexibility, recognising the role of individual, social, cultural and contextual factors in how a person grieves. Ambivalence and difficulties in a relationship, for example, influence grieving and adaptation to loss. Research has shown that widow(er)s who had experienced conflict or an unhappy marriage, initially seem to cope well with their bereavement but, as time goes on, they seemed unable to progress. This could be because they mourn 'not only the marriage that was but also for the marriage that could have been' (Parkes & Weiss, 1983, p. 122).

Most bereaved people, like Nora, manage to make the considerable emotional and social adjustments required of them without any significant mental health problems. Spouses typically show great resourcefulness, personal strength and adaptability after the loss of their partner. Those people experiencing higher levels of distress, such as anxiety or depression, experience gradual improvement in the first year and, after two years, reach a level of functioning similar to those who have not been bereaved (McKiernan, 1996). A significant minority of bereaved people are at risk of physical and mental health problems. Many organisations offer support to the bereaved, but information regarding availability and access needs to be made known to both service-providers and the general public (Kenny, 2004).

Working with bereaved people can be very stressful. It can remind the professional of their own (or potential) losses, grief for which, if unresolved, can make caring for others experiencing loss even more difficult as the professionals' own pain is to the fore hindering their ability to empathise with those grieving. It also raises issues surrounding one's own mortality and the inevitability of death which some people can find frightening and anxious.

Loneliness
The psychological state that results from 'a sense of deprivation in one's social relationships' (Murphy and Kupshik, 1992, p. 3) is another of Nora's concerns. Loneliness is experienced when a person is dissatisfied with their present network of social relationships and feels unable to improve them. Rook (1984) defined it as:

... an enduring condition of emotional distress that arises when a
person feels estranged from, misunderstood, or rejected by others
and/or lacks appropriate social partners for desired activities,
particularly activities that provide a sense of social integration and
opportunities for emotional intimacy.

(p. 1391)

Weiss (1973) distinguished between 'social' and 'emotional' loneliness.
Social loneliness originates from the absence of a network of social
relationships or from feeling 'left out' and 'not belonging'. Emotional
loneliness on the other hand, is experienced as an aching emptiness, having
its genesis in a lack, or loss, of a close, intimate attachment to another person.

Transport may have been a problem for Nora when she lived in the
countryside. This is a problem shared by many older people that contributes
to loneliness. Treacey and colleagues (2005) reported that older people
who have no access to transport, who are aged 85 or over, or who perceive
their health as poor are significantly more likely to experience loneliness.
Social interaction is critical for reducing loneliness. Irish research has
indicated that nearly two-thirds (64.6 per cent) of older people talk with
their neighbours most days while just over a quarter (28.1 per cent) talk
with their neighbours once or twice a week. Over two-thirds (67.8 per cent)
meet friends or relatives most days of the week with a quarter (25.5 per
cent) meeting friends or relatives only one to two times per week. Over a
quarter (27 per cent) of older people, especially those in urban areas, belong
to a club or organisation, compared with just under half (45.9 per cent) of
the rest of the population.

Nora's children have tried to encourage her to join a club or class.
Community activities, accessible transport and lifelong learning courses can
all help alleviate loneliness, isolation and anxiety. Local initiatives, based on
local knowledge, can play an important role in developing the social capital
necessary to promote better mental health and well-being in local
communities (O'Shea & Connolly, 2003).

Health and well-being
Another striking feature of this scenario is the impact of physical illness on
a person's well-being. Nora appears to experience relatively good health
whereas her friend, Paula, has poor health. Well-being refers to general,
everyday mental and physical health. It is multifaceted incorporating the
absence of distress, happiness, life-satisfaction and health.

Irish research has shown that a quarter (25.6 per cent) of older people
feel constrained by a long-term illness, health problem or disability. Just

under half (43.6 per cent) of older people suffer from a chronic physical or mental health problem and this is more common with advancing age (Layte et al., 1999). Nora is quite active and not constrained severely by illness or functional disability. This is quite typical among older people today. Research by Garavan and colleagues (2001) has found low levels of functional disability in the community. Over three quarters of older people living in the community are self-sufficient.

Independent living
'Independence' refers to being free from control or influence, having opportunities to think and act without reference to another person, including a willingness to incur a degree of calculated risk. This scenario also presents the contrast of older people living on their own (Nora) in contrast to those living in residential care (Paula). Nora clearly values being independent. Remaining at home for as long as possible is the preferred option of many older people and declared government policy (Kenny, 2004). Many older people live independently in their own home in relatively good health (Brenner & Shelly, 1998) despite the ageist view that old age is a time of dependency and needing care. Irish research suggests that the majority (three-quarters or more) of older people report receiving emotional, practical and informational support most of the time (Garavan et al., 2001).

Interestingly, the ability to cope with living alone varies according to the stage of life and age at which one comes to live alone. Those who first live alone in their forties and fifties appear to be better able to cope than those who came to be alone when they were in old age (Daly & O'Connor, 1984). It seems, then, that older people fall into two groups in terms of their experience of living alone. The first, consisting largely of people who have not been alone for very long, are generally negative about the experience. For most of these people, however, mainly women, it was the death of a spouse or another close relative that caused them to be alone. The effect of such a traumatic experience was exacerbated by the fact that it also deprived them of their lifelong caring and housekeeping role. The second group, mostly men, are generally positive in their attitudes to living alone. While they admit that there are difficulties, they refuse to be overcome by them. The attitudes of these people are best described as stoical and fatalistic (ibid.).

Psychological issues highlighted in this practice scenario include: psychology of ageing, self-efficacy, friendship and family psychology, including grandparenthood.

PROFESSIONAL PERSPECTIVE

The NCAOP recognises the need for debate at a national level on the place of older people in Irish society. Central to such a debate they identify:

> ... the need to consider and agree as a society the respective roles of the state, the family, the community and the individual in maintaining and developing the independence, self-fulfilment and participation of older people in society while assuring the care and dignity of those older people who are most frail and vulnerable.
> (National Council on Ageing and Older People 2005, p. 9)

Where a debate of this kind would place the role of the professional social care worker is still unclear. Traditionally, care of older people has been based on a medical model, responding to health issues and taking account of social factors only as they impact on the health of the 'patient'. In recent years, there has been a gradually increasing emphasis on the achievement of positive, healthy, well, active or successful ageing (Bowling, 2005, p. 6). This shift in emphasis has begun to impact on policy statements in Ireland, but the main non-medical supports for older people are delivered by voluntary carers, and families, friends and neighbours. Doyle & Timonen (2007) summarised the care in home care provision for older people as follows:

Sector	Public	Private	Non-profit
Primary focus	Personal care	Personal care with domestic work	Domestic work
Care worker titles	Health care assistant	Private agency care worker	Home help

It is interesting to note that there is no mention of social care work in this table, but rather a strong emphasis on meeting physical and health care needs.

In our example, Nora's situation highlights the range of needs that can exist for an older person aside from health and physical care. Her quality of life has diminished as she has become older and her independence has lessened. The professional interviewed in relation to this scenario was a staff nurse in a day care and sheltered housing project. Her comments on the scenario were focused not on health issues but on how Nora's particular circumstances need specific supports to ensure that she remains connected to her community and independent in her living choices. This sense of connectedness and independence was echoed by the service-user interviewed. The interviewee, a woman who described herself as being 'in the early stages of Alzheimer's', stated, 'Like Nora, I prefer to live at home on my own than in a nursing home. I like my independence and value my privacy.' This service-user went on to say that her doctor and psychologist suggested she attend the day care centre 'to bring me out of myself'.

By combining the wider context discussion with the comments on the example, a role for professional social care begins to emerge. That role is based on promoting quality of life, or Q.O.L. 'Q.O.L. theoretically encompasses the individual's physical health, psychological well-being and functioning, independence, control over life, material circumstances and the external environment' (Bowling, 2005, p. 7). The professional social care approach must be to promote the quality of life of the individual. The Alzheimer's Society of Ireland promotes what they term 'person-centred care' in which 'sufferers and carers are placed at the centre of the care service, and the rights of the person with dementia are respected so that they are actively involved in making decisions about their lives' (Murphy et al., in O'Connor & Murphy 2006, p. 303). This approach may be a useful starting point in defining the role of the social care worker in meeting the needs of *all* older people in independent living circumstances.

Key skills
Promoting independent living for older people involves a number of key professional social care skills. These skills can be identified under three headings:

1. Person-centred approach;
2. Practical helping and support; and
3. Integration.

Person-centred approach
The needs of older people are specific to each individual. Building and maintaining a meaningful professional relationship between worker and service-user involves patience, acceptance and perseverance. These are underlying attitudes demanding that the worker give attention to how they communicate – not just to what is said but *how* it is said. 'Unconditional positive regard and non-possessive warmth' (Miley et al., 2004) involve communication of respect, listening to opinions, communicating cordially and honouring cultural difference. The service-user interviewed about this scenario referred to kindness. 'They [the worker] should be kind, you have

to be if you have to do things like change a person's pad, you can't just turn up your nose and say, "I'm not doing that."' Treating the person as an individual and communicating this is at the heart of maintaining their dignity and sense of self-worth.

Practical help and support
'Help me to help myself' is how the same woman put it. Listening with your eyes as well as ears can mean that the social care worker needs to develop heightened observational skills. Being able to identify where, when and to what extent a person needs practical support lessens the need for the service-user to 'ask for' everything. This is important in maintaining the person's sense of independence. It also involved training in practical skills such as 'lifting and handling', household maintenance and perhaps even basic DIY!

Social support
The professional interviewed identified loneliness and isolation as being the most striking feature of Nora's case. According to Nies and Berman (2007):

> All services, including health, social care, housing, transport, social security, education, leisure and other community facilities, should provide the best possible opportunity for people to continue to lead the lives they want, whatever their age.
>
> (p. 4)

In the case of older people accessing or benefiting from some, or all, of these kinds of services may change as their own circumstances evolve. The role of the social care worker here is to provide accurate and clear information, support with form-filling and need-assessment and to advocate for rights and entitlements at whatever time this help should be required.

Professional issues highlighted in this practice scenario include: person-centred care, quality of life promotion, dignity, professional communication and observational skills.

PART TWO

RIGHTS

A Brief Introduction to Rights

Any discussion on rights can easily descend – or ascend – into a philosophical debate on how we as humans can best share space on this 'third rock from the sun'. The rights theme that covers the next three scenarios of this book, however, focuses on how social care workers engage with and promote the rights of the people using their services. This introduction discusses briefly the definitions of rights, the recognition and protection of rights, and the role of the social care profession in the promotion of the rights of marginalised individuals and groups.

RIGHTS: A DEFINITION

Thomas Hobbes (1588–1679) asserted that a right is a liberty, that a person is at liberty to do something or say something when there is no obligation not to do so. This starting point links rights to freedom – freedom from coercion by governments or interference by others. Other definitions emphasise duties, legal obligations, individual or state power and the competitive nature of rights. In short, rights are usually discussed in terms of human rights, civil rights or legal rights. Wellman (2002) works towards a definition of what a right is by trying to include all its aspects: interest, claim, duty, liberty, power, permission and judicial. He fails to create a single definition but comes instead to the conclusion that:

> ... rights have three fundamental characteristics (1) they are permissive for their possessor ... (2) rights imply duties of other individuals ... (3) rights are protected or secured to the individual by society.
>
> (p. 251)

Although the concept of rights can be traced back to ancient civilisations, the inscription of rights (i.e. their written and acknowledged place in national and international laws) is relatively recent. The American and French revolutions produced the Declaration of Independence in 1776 and the Declaration of the Rights of Man and the Citizen in 1789 respectively. More recent declarations have expanded on their main themes of the protection of human rights based on individual rights to life and liberty. After the Second World War, there was worldwide recognition that norms of international behaviour needed to be expressed as rights, leading to the United Nations Declaration of Human Rights in 1948. Charleton (2007) points out that this declaration in 1976 'amended and divided into a list of Civil and Political Rights and Economic, Social and Cultural Rights'. He goes on to say: 'It is the economic, social and cultural rights that are of particular relevance to social care' (ibid., p. 70). Perhaps it is impossible to define precisely what 'a right' is, but a useful working definition is provided by Hinman (1997) (cited in Cussen, 2005): 'Rights are a contemporary way of assessing morality or another way to talk about how people ought to be treated' (p. 88).

Ireland ratified the UN Convention on the Rights of the Child in 1992, illustrating how individual countries engage with such international declarations. The government is obliged to ensure that the minimum standards set by this convention are met. The Human Rights Commission Act 2000 confers a wide ranging competence on Ireland's Human Rights Commission to promote and protect human rights defined as follows:

1. the rights, liberties and freedoms conferred on, or guaranteed to, persons by the Constitution, and
2. the rights, liberties or freedoms conferred on, or guaranteed by any agreement, treaty or convention to which the state is a party.

(Office of the UNHCR, 2007)

RIGHTS-BASED SOCIAL CARE WORK

We have concentrated so far on what rights are and how they are expressed. In an ideal world, social justice would prevail, giving all people equal rights and equal opportunity to participate fully in society. They would have equal protection but, also, equal obligations and access to social benefit. However, we do not live in an ideal world. Social care work is often provided for individuals and groups whose rights are not fully acknowledged, respected or protected. There may be a lack of clarity about people's rights or even judgements or conditions attached to individual access to rights. It is impossible to work with people whose rights are infringed upon without having a professional responsibility to understand and challenge the source of this injustice, whether that source is person-based or structural.

Charleton (2007) provides useful examples of where social care workers can come across issues relating to rights in providing care. He includes a scenario of a family from an ethnic minority – the Travelling Community – experiencing discrimination in trying to get accommodation (p. 66). In responding to the needs of such a family, the social care worker engages at a number of levels: the immediate or 'micro' level with the family itself; at the local community level or 'meso' level with other professionals and community representatives; and at the structural or 'macro' level with society at a national or international level. It is the professional responsibility of the social care worker to be aware of, understand and address the human rights of the family at all three levels.

The scenarios that follow in this section reflect aspects of the social care worker's professional roles and responsibilities in protecting and promoting rights. 'Rights corresponding to human needs have to be upheld and fostered, and they embody the justification and motivation for social (care) work action' (UN Centre for Human Rights 1994, p. 8). Advocacy of such rights must therefore be an integral part of the work. This advocacy role is explored in Practice Scenario Five. An interdisciplinary approach in a community childcare work setting illustrates, in Practice Scenario Six, the importance of promoting service-users' rights at a wider community and structural level. This can only be achieved if the worker is informed not only about existing national and international human rights instruments, but also about how the individual and societal structures interact, especially when injustice and marginalisation have occurred. The third and final scenario in this section focuses on working in partnership with service-users. This is an empowering approach and is key to ensuring that the rights of the service-user, the worker and others involved in the evolving situation are protected. The partnership model can involve the challenge of dealing with competing rights, of educating about the responsibilities attached to rights and of exploring our own values and their impact on our professional work.

The protection and promotion of rights is an aspect of social care work in which, perhaps more than any other, the worker's knowledge, skill and personal values combine in day-to-day professional practice. The close and ongoing professional relationships that exist between service-user and worker in the social care context often give the worker a unique insight into a world where rights are not implemented in daily life. When one strips away the legal and philosophical discourses, as Freeman (1992) does, one is left with a clear and unambiguous truth: 'Rights are about doing, acting

within relationships, and are only as useful as their implementation permits.'
(Freeman, 1992 in Flekhog & Kaufman, 1997, p. 8).

– 4 –

Advocacy

Homelessness in Ireland:
People in Ireland considered homeless may include those who are:
- sleeping rough
- staying in emergency hostels or refuges
- staying in bed and breakfast accommodation on a temporary basis
- staying temporarily with friends or family because they have nowhere else to go
- staying in squats (occupying a building illegally)

The term 'out-of-home' is often used to refer to people who have nowhere to live. This term recognises the fact that you may have a home that you cannot return to for whatever reason, and that if you have no home currently, that the situation is not permanent.
- Most homeless women in Dublin are young mothers who are caring for their children in unsuitable private rented accommodation with low levels of support.*
- The two most common reasons for entry into homelessness are a lack of affordable accommodation and domestic violence. Just 13 per cent of those experiencing violence availed of specialised refuge services for 'battered' women. Fear of retaliation was the most common reason given for delaying or failing to seek help.*

A recent report, *Counted In*, published by the Homeless Agency, indicates that the total homeless population reported for the Dublin area in 2005 was 2,015. This 2,015 figure consisted of 1,552 adults and 463 children. The then government indicated that they would be providing €45 million in national funding for homeless accommodation and related services the following year.

*source Children's Research Centre, Trinity College, Dublin and Health Services Research Centre, Royal College of Surgeons.

Practice Scenario 4

Setting: Homeless Support Agency

Mary and her three children have been homeless for the past two and a half years. They became homeless having fled domestic violence, spending periods of time in refuges and bed and breakfasts. Although the violence and subsequent homelessness is the worst of their situation, Mary can't help but think that she has also lost much of her social network and self-respect. Prior to leaving the family home, Mary was considered by most as comfortable and even privileged. Mary was raised in a middle-class family and married her husband who came from a working-class background. Working to put her husband through business school, Mary was proud of her husband's ambition and early promotions through the ranks. It wasn't long before her husband was offered a partnership in a local company. Mary thought that life would be as she had dreamed, especially when she found herself pregnant with their first child, whose birth was followed closely by a second child. Things changed, however, when her husband's company failed and he became unemployed. Unable to find work, he began to drink heavily and then became extremely critical of Mary's child-rearing and housekeeping. Trying to make ends meet seemed impossible; Mary had never wanted for anything and she had little life experience that prepared her for this new challenge. When Mary was pregnant with their third child, her husband's drinking became obsessive. At the first instance of domestic violence, Mary just cried. The second time, she went with the children to her mother's and returned home the following day. The third time, she called the Gardaí. The fourth time, she went with the children to a women's refuge for a week. She returned there after the fifth incident and stayed away from the home. The fact that the children were increasingly becoming the targets for the assaults led her to finally leave. The older children have been attending school, but have a high absentee rate and Mary has noticed that their behaviour with other children has become more 'rough' and manipulative. She wonders if their living environment over the past months is changing their attitudes as well. Mary has the third child with her during the day and uses the local community centre crèche facility whenever possible. They are on the priority housing waiting list and have been offered a house, but Mary is refusing to move in because the house in question is too close to her husband's family and she fears for her safety. The local authority says that if she refuses this offer, she will move down the waiting list and it may be two years before she is considered for another property. She spends most of her time attending meetings with housing officers, community welfare officers and social workers. She feels ashamed and embarrassed talking to these people about what has happened to her and her family.

They must all think I am a useless mother. To have stayed with him for so long after what he did to me and the children and to have no home for my children. They are there in their fancy clothes feeling sorry for me. I wish I knew more, what to do and say. I can't even work a computer so I'm never going to be able to get a job.

She feels no one is working on her behalf and that she is just a number in a huge bureaucratic nation. Her biggest worry is about the welfare of her children in the short and long term. Mary's family are aware of all that's happened over the past year but they have not been quick to become involved. Mary is hurt that they have not offered to help her financially, especially for the children's sake.

For further consideration...

1. The impact of social structures on the lives of marginalised families.
2. The effects of domestic violence on individual members of the family.
3. The advocacy role of the social care worker in responding to the needs of the family.

SOCIOLOGICAL PERSPECTIVE

Family structure and breakdown

Sociologists differ on definitions of the family in society. They generally agree, however, that the family is not easily characterised, and no single definition accurately describes the domestic relationships and arrangements to which all individuals and groups belong. Families are an important symbol of collective identity, unity and security and many social scientists see the family as the 'natural' basis of society (O'Connor, 1998). Most sociologists would agree that in order to understand any particular society, one must attempt to understand the role and function of the family in that society, because within the family framework, power and equality issues are realised.

As well as having a range of family structures, Irish families also reflect an array of family roles. Sociology has approached the family through various perspectives, with the functionalist, class and feminist analysis being regularly considered when attempting to understand the purpose and effects of family membership upon Irish society. O'Connor (1998, p. 89) states that: 'The family in Ireland, as elsewhere, has been identified as an important symbol of collective identity, unity and security.' This role and definition must, however, be reconsidered, as traditional family functions are regularly transferred from the domestic sphere to public social institutions (e.g. education, social and economic welfare services, gardaí, community and religious groups). In addition, family membership is no longer limited to the mother, father, children and perhaps extended family, but includes separated parents, lone parents, step-parents, long-term partners, step-siblings and so forth.

Domestic violence and child abuse have always existed in families, but only recently in Ireland has the volume of violence and abuse has been publicly identified and considered. This scrutiny has resulted in several changes in legislation, giving the Irish state the right and obligation to intervene on behalf of the individuals who are victimised. (Refer, for example, to the Domestic Violence Act 1996; Status of Children Act 1987; Adoption Act 1988; Child Care Act 1991). Despite the legislative support, further research indicates that even when women report levels of injury and violence, they are still faced with the prospect of poverty, homelessness and, in some cases, the loss of their children (Kelleher Associates, 2001; O'Connor, 2004).

In the practice scenario above, Mary and her children have been living in a violent home with several social consequences resulting from their exposure to physical and emotional abuse. Mary is experiencing a breakdown in what sociologists consider one of the primary social institutions that holds society together – the family. In addition, Mary is facing the loss of her 'social network' and local support from relationships and contacts within the community. She is deprived of arrangements that provide 'social glue' and compensation for emotional conflict. Sociologists realise that the causes and prevention of violence in the home rests at several different levels – namely, individual relationships, access to community services and societal values and norms.

In terms of Mary's individual relationships, she and her children experienced abuse when her husband became obsessed with alcohol and subsequently, by his domination of the family. Mary's community services (e.g. the local crèche facility, social housing, gardaí) have left her feeling isolated and dependent upon meagre provisions and insufficient social supports. She and her children are at risk in a society that has failed to protect her against violence and abuse. No matter what angle one takes in attempting to address violence against women and children, a key factor to ensuring long-term change is for women and children to be central to the development, delivery and evaluation of service provision.

Social capital

As a result of domestic violence, family breakdown and involuntary homelessness, Mary and her children have been isolated from meaningful activity in their local community. Research conducted by Coleman (1966, 1988) found that the impact of communities was a source of social capital that could counterbalance the economic and social disadvantages endured by families living in adverse circumstances. Social capital works at a very basic level, using an individual's networks to renegotiate situations and challenging circumstances, changing them from private difficulties into public concerns. Social capital is not created by an individual or even within a particular social structure. Rather, it is created when people form networks with others based on trust and reciprocation. Bauman (1999) states that:

> People who have been excluded and isolated are easily stripped of any sense of power and agency. They internalise their experiences and blame themselves for their exclusion … Society tends to exclude or stereotype the least powerful in society…

When people stop blaming themselves or accepting the labels of personal inadequacy imposed by the outside world, they can begin to frame what Woliver (1996) calls 'narratives of resistance'. The core view of social capital is that relationships matter (Field, 2003) and that benefits result from social connections. According to Halpern (2005), the family is a significant variant in social capital. Early attachments have a significant impact on social skills, relationships and expectations, and help to explain the causes of advantages and disadvantages for family members.

Mary has communicated feelings of inadequacy and hopelessness, fearing what others might think of her and she has expressed her shame and embarrassment. She looks at the consequences of her husband's violence as being her fault, and blames herself for what she sees as a bleak future. Mary has not been gainfully employed since she had children, and has suspended the development of her professional profile and marketability. Consequences of the marriage breakdown have left her vulnerable and without financial independence. Equally, Mary's children have been negatively affected by their father's abuse and appear now to be demonstrating a lack of trust in and connection with the adult world. Poor school attendance and continued homelessness increase their likelihood of creating a negative spiral as they form relationships with other vulnerable young people who lack more conventional forms of social capital (see McCarthy, Hagan & Martin, 2002). In the practice scenario, a decreasing amount of social capital is available for Mary and her children. Unless immediate and positive intervention is made, there will likely be damaging consequences for their lives and social relationships.

Social class, status and mobility

Having come from a middle-class background prior to her marriage, Mary redefined her social network and community by marrying her husband, combining her middle- and his working-class environments. By working hard to support her husband's business education and progression, both Mary and her husband moved from a working-class environment into to a middle-class social category. Now homeless and living in shelters, Mary is distressed as she finds herself in the 'underclass', a social category living with multiple social disadvantages and dependent on state welfare benefits. It should be noted however that MacDonald and Marsh (2000) argue that unemployment and job insecurity have become common working-class experiences making the 'underclass' an invalid social culture or categorisation. Taking this into account, in the practice scenario, Mary is currently marginalised and excluded from mainstream society, and recognises that she has experienced downward social mobility. Previously, Mary was comfortably within a middle-class social category; now she finds herself displaced, living on the edge of society, attempting to make ends meet on a daily basis and becoming increasingly isolated from mainstream society.

Advocacy and empowerment

Advocacy is a means of empowering people by supporting them to assert their views and claim their entitlements and, where necessary, representing and negotiating on their behalf. Social exclusion, individual problems, or low levels of literacy combined with bureaucratic complexity can leave some people vulnerable and at a disadvantage in claiming their entitlements or getting the services they need (Citizens Information Board, 2008; Weafer & Woods, 2003). Advocates can intervene by enabling, representing or even lobbying for people, making it possible for them to speak for themselves or to have their case heard. From a sociological and social care perspective, Mary and her children are in need of assistance that will identify facts and options, and help to move them towards social inclusion and community reintegration. By examining Mary's web of relationships and interests, a quality of support can be established that will begin to reverse any exclusion that has arisen as a result of her long-term domestic circumstances. Improved provision of social services in health, education, housing and child protection can increase Mary's social stability and restore feelings of self-worth in her and in her children. By working together, welfare agencies, informal social networks and each family member will promote a partnership that offers flexibility for all stakeholders and 'levels the playing field' for Mary and her children. Most importantly, however, is the central involvement of Mary and each of her children in this process. By respecting their choices and valuing their involvement in decision-making, the outcomes are more likely to meet the expectations of all parties and increase the positive effect of considered intervention.

Sociological issues highlighted in this practice scenario include:
- **Intervention that empowers service-users and increases self-respect.**
- **Social isolation and the role of community.**
- **Decision-making.**
- **Social networking and social capital.**
- **Social status.**
- **Social mobility.**

PSYCHOLOGICAL PERSPECTIVE
In looking at this practice scenario from a psychological perspective, a number of issues stand out for consideration. Firstly, why does domestic violence occur? Secondly, what are the effects of such violence on the partner and the family? Thirdly, how can Mary and the children be helped? Before these questions are addressed, it is important to consider what domestic violence is and its prevalence in Ireland. Psychology as a discipline has a lot to contribute to our understanding of the relationship dynamics in domestic violence, as well as the impact of such violence upon family members, emotionally, mentally and socially.

Prevalence and forms of domestic abuse
Statistics from callers to the Women's Aid helpline across 2006 indicate that 60 per cent of callers reported emotional abuse, 25 per cent physical abuse, 10 per cent financial abuse and 5 per cent sexual abuse (Women's Aid, 2006). See the Professional Perspective in this chapter for further details.

It is also worth noting that with the intention of ensuring a woman's compliance to their wishes, abusive men seek actively to isolate women from any possible sources of support, such as family, friends and community, and many women are prevented from accessing paid employment.

Irish research suggests that 18 per cent of women have been subjected to at least one form of violence at some time in their lives by a current or former partner. The violence reported included mental cruelty (13 per cent), actual physical violence (10 per cent), threatened physical violence (9 per cent), sexual violence (4 per cent) and property damage (2 per cent) (Kelleher et al., 1995). Still other research has reported that approximately one in seven Irish women and one in sixteen Irish men have experienced severe abuse. This study also highlighted the greater susceptibility for domestic violence with parenthood:

Those who ever had children face over three times the odds of severe abuse compared to those without children. This pattern was found for both men and women and is unrelated to the age of the children or to the number of children. The greater vulnerability associated with parenthood could be due to a number of factors, including the stresses of parenthood or the greater difficulty in leaving a relationship when there are children involved.

(Watson & Parsons, 2005, p. 24)

The link between men's abuse of women and child abuse has been well established by research (Cleaver et al., 1999; Hester et al., 2000), highlighting that concerns for child protection be foremost in any domestic violence case (Holt, 2003). Children are often assaulted as part of the violence, either as a tactic used by the man to further control their mother or when they actively try to intervene to protect their mother (Hogan & O'Reilly, 2007). In 2006, there were 1,942 specific incidents of child abuse by the violent partner disclosed by callers to the Women's Aid Helpline. These incidents included the abuser urinating on the child, the child being kicked in the stomach, being taught to be violent and being exposed to pornography, including child pornography (Women's Aid, 2007).

Why does domestic violence occur?

Many psychological explanations have been put forward to explain domestic violence. Some focus on individual factors, such as psychopathology and child-rearing experiences.

For example, an abusive family background is known to be a contributing factor in perpetuating the cycle of domestic violence in the abuser, showing how violence of this kind can be learned. Forensic psychology research in the UK with a sample of convicted domestic violence offenders identified several risk factors. These included anti-social personality disorders, witnessing domestic violence in childhood, disrupted attachment patterns, high levels of interpersonal dependency and jealousy, a lack of empathy and macho attitudes condoning domestic violence (Gilchrist et al., 2003).

Other explanations have focused on features of the violent relationship. Research into male violence in intimate relationships has identified the key roles of power and control, with men using a wide range of abusive and coercive tactics to exert power and control over their partner's life. Power is seen by many to be linked to gender inequality and argued by many feminists to explain why women are more likely to be victims of domestic violence. Feelings of jealousy often accompany a sense of loss of control

over a partner and may trigger a
partner, usually the man, places th
than more democratic, egalitari
influence is shared on a more eq
they used violence on their partne
through to their partners has t
Alcohol and drug misuse, as w
commonly cited as precipitating

Other psychological explanati
violence as a process rather th;
influence. Exchange/Social con
and 'costs' of being violent and on 'internai ()....
self-regulation) and 'external' controls (laws, loss of respect by oiiiii.,
called 'inner' and 'outer' containment. Central to these theories is the
contention that people are violent when the costs of being violent (risk of
social ostracism, a violent response, imprisonment) are *lesser* than the rewards
(such as control, power and esteem). In essence, people are violent because
they *can* be. Thus, social controls, such as legislation and social interventions,
as well as personal controls, such as a strong moral consciousness and
integration into the extended family, community and conventional society,
reduce the likelihood of domestic violence (Gelles, 1997).

A systemic approach to domestic violence offers a useful framework
through which to understand the complexity of domestic violence. It allows
for a more sophisticated analysis of domestic violence, looking at factors
which can help to protect potential victims of domestic violence and
interactions within the family system and across wider systemic levels, such
as community (e.g. the isolation of the family unit) and culture (norms,
values, legislation) (Cooper & Vetere, 2005). In this practice scenario for
example, it appears that Mary's family of origin has provided little support.
They may have been pushed away by Mary's partner and by Mary and her
husband's relationship. This isolation of the family unit, distanced from the
extended family, is found in many cases of family abuse. It can be seen in
'The Kilkenny Incest Case ' and is also portrayed in the book *Sophia's Story*
by Susan McKay (1998).

What are the effects of domestic violence?

Women who experience domestic violence are affected on many levels. Not
only do they experience physical injuries, poor self-esteem, depression and
other mental health problems, but they are also at risk of addictions and
other health problems as a result of violence, including a wide range of
gynaecological problems (Garcia-Moreno, 2004). More significantly, they

...sed by their experience which may be not as keenly
...ysical injuries (Lewis Herman, 1992).
...mestic violence invariably experience powerlessness, feeling
...othing about the violence they experience. This 'numbing'
...n result in a feeling of being 'trapped' with failure to see or
... help available to them. It may also hinder them from seeing the
...sed to any children in the family from the violent partner. Cases of
...ly abuse such as the Kilkenny Incest case and the West of Ireland case,
...escribed in *Sophia's Story* present accounts of how disempowered mothers
as victims of domestic violence may become. These cases also highlight the
degree of power exerted by the dominant, authoritarian and violent father.
In contrast, male victims of domestic violence often blame themselves for
the violence inflicted upon them and feelings of self-blame, guilt and shame
can hinder them from seeking help (McKeown & Kidd, 2000), feelings
they share with many female victims of domestic violence.

In our practice scenario, it is clear that Mary was prompted to leave and
seek help because she was aware of the potential effects that witnessing
violence may have on her children and, more immediately, because of the
increased violence against the children. This shows that she is capable of
looking after the welfare of her children.

Much psychological research has looked at the effects of domestic violence
on children. Studies have identified the negative impact of children witnessing
violence towards their mothers. Distress, depression and poor mental health
are some of the main effects (Brandon & Lewis, 1996). Children
understandably find it difficult to cope with such 'frightening and terrorising
experiences' (Cleaver et al., 1999, p. 91). Chaos in children's lives, a direct
result of the violence, can have its own significant consequences. Instances of
unplanned pregnancy, drug and alcohol abuse, behavioural problems,
physical health problems and dropping out of school have all been attributed
to domestic violence, according to one Irish study (Hogan & O'Reilly,
2007). Other Irish research has illuminated the role of domestic violence in
contributing to youth homelessness (Mayock & Carr, 2008).

How can victims of domestic violence be helped?

Psychologically, empowerment can and should be applied at the level of
the individual, child or adult. A professional approach that values
empowerment would be useful in working with Mary. Professionals should
make Mary aware that they are there to help her and to empower her to
help herself. Such an approach may move her to regain a greater sense of
power over her life. Psychological empowerment 'integrates perception of
personal control, participation with others to achieve goals and a critical

awareness of the factors that hinder or enhance one's effort to exert control in one's life' (Zimmerman & Warschausky, 1998, p. 4). It consists of:

- *intrapersonal elements*: how a person thinks about themselves, self-esteem, motivation and personal values;
- *interactional elements:* how a person thinks about others, their family, professionals and so forth; and
- *behavioural elements*: actions by the person undertaken to influence others and social institutions and organizations.

(Zimmerman, 1995)

Peled and colleagues (2000) argue that an empowerment-based perspective should present returning to or staying with the violent man as a legitimate choice, one which does not prevent tackling the violence from within the relationship once safety planning and coping strategies have been worked out. This does however pose professionals with challenges and requires a complete turnaround in thinking for the professional with more experience in encouraging a woman to get out of or stay away from such a relationship. This practice scenario also highlights the need for professional sensitivity and self-awareness; here it is apparent that Mary has been further hurt, ashamed and embarrassed in her dealings with social care professionals. A large number of social care professionals at any one meeting can also be intimidating for a person or persons in need of help (Buckley, 2002).

Some of the practice guidelines advocated by O'Connor & Wilson (2002) for Women's Aid include:

- Maximise the woman's safety. Responses and interventions must maximise women's and children's safety and must always seek to avoid increased risk and danger.
- Understand the trauma of violence and support a woman's increasing autonomy with interventions and responses that are respectful and supportive of a woman's attempts to regain power and control over her life.
- Be informed and knowledgeable about the rights, entitlements and options for women and ensure that referral is appropriate and responsible.
- Advocate for the woman's rights. A commitment to active advocacy means ensuring that your power, skills, knowledge and expertise are at the service of the woman.

These guidelines emphasise how important it is for the worker to take account of the psychological trauma that results from living with domestic violence. The mix of practical and direct assistance needs to ensure that the person being helped is central to all decision-making and actions.

In working with children, it is important to note that the greatest practical and emotional support for most children in domestic violence situations comes from their siblings, and then from their mothers, rather than from professionals (Hogan & O'Reilly, 2007). Children are understandably more at ease with people they are familiar with. The crisis and often short-term nature of refuge services is a barrier to working effectively with children who have experienced domestic violence because children don't have time to build up a relationship with professionals and because their everyday routines are 'normal' life is upset (ibid.). In addition, apart from refuges, there is a lack of community-based services and/or community care social work response in Ireland for families in which there is domestic violence. Not all women or children (and certainly not all teenagers) want a refuge-based service. Many would prefer community-based supports, such as drop-in centres, where they could get support and advice (ibid.).

Research in Ireland by Hogan and O'Reilly (2007) found that most young children interviewed in refuges (albeit a small sample) spoke of missing their fathers, despite their violent behaviour. Many of these children's mothers also felt that access with their fathers was important for the children.

Teenagers, on the other hand, did not report missing their fathers or wanting access visits arranged. Some of these teenagers spoke of living with a 'control freak', a man who tried to control everything they did, in the form of threats and derogatory talk about women. Many teenagers reported years of witnessing and overhearing violence. Overhearing the violence was an enormous stress for some of them, as they could only imagine what was happening to their mother.

Many blocks have been identified in the responses of professionals to cases of domestic violence (Holt, 2003). Firstly, a professional's own value system may be an issue; their response to a case may be affected by a dominant belief that the family should stay together for the sake of the children, manifested in a disbelief of the severity of the problem. Secondly, professionals may not adequately identify or respond to abused women on the basis of information made available to them. The violence may not be seen as early as it could be from information gathered about the family.

Thirdly, professionals often underestimate or disregard the seriousness of the situation, possibly due to a lack of knowledge of the dynamics of domestic violence. A systemic model of the family helps to contextualise the family's situation, identifying the contributory factors to the escalation of violence. In addition, women must not be perceived solely as passive victims, but as resilient people who need alternatives in addition to therapy. Care should be taken not to re-victimise women or to undermine their own role in the process and potential for self-advocacy. A lack of clarity in policy and practice guidelines may also result in professional confusion regarding how to respond, in addition to the block caused by the sheer case-load experienced by professionals in the field.

Finally, abused women are often afraid to seek help for fear that their children may be taken from them and into care. They may worry about professionals asking how, if they cannot protect themselves, can they protect their children? Another block identified by Holt (2003) is the professional's own fear of violent men resulting in cases being avoided ('pushed to the bottom of the bundle'), or the men not being challenged. Professionals' lack training and understanding of the psychological impact of domestic violence may mean that they are simply not skilled enough to work with intimidation and aggression.

Psychological issues highlighted in this practice scenario include:
- **Understanding the impact of domestic violence on individual family members.**
- **The blocks that may hinder the worker/service-user relationship when domestic violence is a dominant issue.**
- **Other psychological issues of concern that may be explored in respect to this scenario include: aggression, self-esteem and Maslow's hierarchy of needs.**

PROFESSIONAL PERSPECTIVE

The interaction between Mary and a social care worker may well occur in an agency focused on advocacy towards securing short- and long-term solutions to homelessness. Finding a place to live is the immediate and urgent need. However, the way in which the agency and the individual worker respond to Mary needs to be sensitive to the reasons for her homelessness. The starting point for this discussion on the professional perspective therefore is a brief description of the types of abuse that occur.

Emotional abuse includes threats to kill, threats to hurt or kill any children, physically aggressive behaviour, such as punching holes in doors and walls, never being called by her own name and being spoken to in derogatory terms. For many women emotional abuse or the threat of violence can be more frightening than actual physical violence (Kelleher & O'Connor, 1995). Mobile phones have been used to send threatening and abusive messages to mothers as well as to children about what their father was going to do to them. (Hogan & O'Reilly, 2007). Many abusers continue to harass their partner after she has left, showing the need for measures such as Barring Orders.

Forms of physical abuse include: being strangled until unconscious, stripped naked and beaten, being punched where it won't 'show', thrown and assaulted. In its most extreme form, the violence may result in homicide. An estimated 40 to more than 70 per cent of homicides of women worldwide are perpetrated by intimate partners, frequently in the context of an abusive relationship (Ellsberg & Heise, 2005).

Sexual abuse includes: being raped, coerced into re-enacting pornography and being forced into prostitution.

Finally, financial abuse includes: being denied access to money, even for household basics, having bank accounts closed to stop the woman leaving and non-payment for child maintenance (Women's Aid, 2006).

Mary's rapid move to homelessness has left her vulnerable, isolated and confused. She feels let down by social service professionals and invisible in a bureaucratic system that treats her as a number rather than as an individual. It is clear, however, that Mary has strong resilience and inner strength with a fearless drive to do what is best for her children and herself. Too often, women regret that they ever broke the silence surrounding their abuse because of the negative consequences and escalated violence they experienced following disclosure. 'The challenge for all practitioners is ensuring that at least one outcome for women, following our intervention is a positive experience of increased support and safety' (O'Connor 1999, p. 9). This discussion will now focus on advocacy and its role in responding to Mary's needs. As a social care skill (or subset of skills) advocacy needs to be viewed as an integral part of the social care profession as a whole.

> When I am working with a woman who has experienced violence I have three eyes. One eye focused on her, one on the man who is invisible to us and controlling and abusing her and one on the institutions which fail to protect her or hold him accountable for his violence and abuse.
>
> (Jean O'Flynn cited in O'Connor & Wilson, 2002)

Mary and her children need reassurance, support and advice when requested. She needs someone to talk to who shows empathy and is not judgemental or bureaucratic.

In Ireland, after a friend or relative, the person to whom a woman experiencing abuse is most likely to disclose to is her GP (Kelleher &

O'Connor, 1995). However, research carried out in doctor's surgeries indicates that few women are asked about domestic violence by their general practitioner (Bradley et al., 2002). This has obvious health implications.

> There is a lack of flexibility demonstrated by the local housing authorities; a lack of assessment of this family's needs; and interventions that appear to have left Mary feeling more worthless and guilty, rather than empowered and supported.
> (Support worker working with people homeless commenting on Mary's situation)

The comment above gets to the heart of the matter: whilst it may be true that Mary's low self-esteem and powerlessness have been caused by her homelessness, these feelings have been compounded by 'the system' in place to respond to her homelessness.

Advocacy comes in many forms (citizens', legal, collective, self- and peer) all with a common aim to 'ensure that people who are in receipt of services have a voice that is respected and valued ... listened to and acknowledged' (Dalrymple & Burke 2006, p. 258). Many women's organisations around the world have advocated for domestic violence to be considered as a human rights issue.

Mary has found herself on the margins of society. In discussing the practice scenario with a young mother who found herself similarly marginalised by homelessness, it became clear that the barriers to gaining a secure foothold in society come from within as well as from a bureaucratic system. She immediately identified with Mary's feeling of isolation and lack of self-worth. 'My support-worker tells me I'm doing a great job. I know I am now but for a long time I thought I wasn't.' So perhaps the first stage of advocacy is to work in partnership with the service-user, addressing low self-esteem and self-worth. This aspect of advocacy work may continue throughout the working relationship.

O'Connor and Murphy (2006) calls for a social care practice that seeks to open dialogue with service-users, that empowers and involves them in representing their own needs and concerns, and in decision-making towards addressing these needs. This approach demands that the social care worker as advocate is not so much the 'voice for' the service-user but an intrinsic element of the 'voice of' the service-user. When asked what might help to bring about an improvement in Mary's situation, the young homeless mother we spoke to again emphasised the partnership approach based on trust and affirmation, the need for 'someone to tell her it's not her fault, that she's doing well and to help her to start planning for the future ... maybe someone just to listen to what Mary wants instead of what everyone else thinks she should do'. She went on to say that at a national level what might help would be 'a government that gives a damn about people like me', adding, 'what about a government made up of people like me'! This last comment raises an interesting question about the extent to which service-users should be involved in planning their own services. Much has been written on the topic (see, for example, Craig, 1998; Pritchard, 2001), but a model of best practice for service-user involvement is presented by Turner, (1997, in Miley et al., 2004) who sums up the work of an organisation in the US called Shaping Our Lives. This influential organisation for people with disabilities draws upon the expertise of service-users. 'Goals include empowering service-users by advocating personal decision-making and control, creating responsive programmes and services, redressing discrimination and social injustice, and promoting social change' (ibid., p. 365).

Table 2.1 Aspects of Advocacy

Characteristics of Advocacy Work	
Finding the Voice	Listening, acknowledging, affirming, working in partnership
Voicing	Rights-based work, understanding the issues, expression/articulation of the issues, empowering clients
Amplifying the Voice	Radicalising, challenging systems, change-/action-oriented

Achieving these goals show the multidimensional nature of advocacy in the social care context. Table 2.1 summarises these dimensions and aligns with them the characteristics of the professional roles associated with each. The voice must always remain that of the service-user.

Professional issues highlighted in this practice scenario include:
- **Looking behind the immediate need presented.**
- **Understanding the advocacy role.**
- **Understanding the advocacy relationship.**
- **Understanding the advocacy process.**

– 5 –

Interdisciplinary Work

The Community Childcare Worker in context

The HSE is a large organisation of over 100,000 people, the job of which it is to run all of the public health services in Ireland. The HSE manages services through a structure designed to put patients and clients at the centre of the organisation. It has three clearly defined interdependent areas: Health and Personal Social Services, Support Services and Reform & Innovation.

Health and Personal Social Services

Health and Personal Social Services are divided into three areas:

- Population Health that promotes and protects the health of the entire population.
- Primary Community and Continuing Care (PCCC) that delivers care in the community.
- National Hospitals Office (NHO) that provides acute hospital and ambulance services.

Primary, Community and Continuing Care services are the point of first contact for people in the community that need to access health and social services in Ireland providing health and personal social services in communities. This includes primary care, mental health, disability, children, youth and families, community hospital, continuing care services, and social inclusion services.

A Community Childcare Worker works with other professionals to enhance the development of children both in the care of the HSE and those who have been identified as being at risk, deprived, disadvantaged or requiring special attention for any of a number of reasons. The HSE Community Care teams in which they work may include GP Out-of-Hours Services, Public Health Nursing, Social Work, Fostering Service, Child

Health, Community Welfare and Psychology. Other professionals on multidisciplinary teams can include teachers, gardaí, probation workers and Youth and Community Workers.

Practice Scenario 5

Setting: Community childcare

Michelle is a childcare worker and works in a community care child protection team. She works alongside social workers and other health and social welfare professionals. She finds team meetings very stressful as the team members often have such different perspectives on cases. Frequently, she feels that she is not heard simply because she is not a child's social worker or GP, even though she has spent more time with the child than others at the meeting. Sometimes she thinks, 'What's the point of me saying anything when they're the ones that will decide what will happen anyhow? What they say goes.' She knows it is important, however, to present all perspectives on a case. When she first started, Michelle had to learn quickly all the abbreviations and jargon used by the GP, psychologist, social workers and others so she could understand what they were talking about. Often, Michelle feels that members in the team fall into regular alliances, siding with the same people on different issues and not giving due regard to the perspectives of others on cases discussed. She also finds it hard to hold different views from those of colleagues with whom she works closely. Michelle feels that they will think she is letting them down if she disagrees with them in front of the others.

It can also be unclear at times where one person's responsibility with a case starts and finishes. Sometimes entire meetings revolve around whose responsibility certain actions are and who knows a case best, which can make meetings very tense and heated. From her past experience, Michelle is aware of how much influence is exerted upon any professional both by the other professionals and by the working relationships with the family members. Carol, a colleague, once said to her that teamwork is much harder than a top-down 'chain of command', because at least with the latter you just go to your line manager and they decide and tell you what to do.

For further consideration...

1. Roles, structure and power in the workplace.
2. Teamwork and team roles.
3. Social care as a profession amongst professions.

Sociological Perspective

There is recognition amongst social care providers that a disjointed approach to service provision is less than effective. Instead, collaboration is the desirable – and in fact essential – model to providing care. By viewing care as a multi-faceted task, partnership becomes an accepted way of working. Colleagues and agency representatives regard interdependency as a strategic and valuable model that shapes best practice, leading to co-operation, trust, altruism and user-centred objectives. In their analysis of child protection practices in Ireland, Buckley et al. (1997) highlight several areas that support coordination amongst professional practitioners from varied disciplines, including the pooling of skills and resources, facilitating each other's work (e.g. flexibility), good communication, mutual support, respect and valuing other's roles, and personal interaction (i.e. social aspects of teamwork).

In the practice scenario above, Michelle is faced with a situation in which she feels that others are failing to recognise her professional skills and contributions. There is an apparent lack of understanding by her colleagues regarding her role and involvement in the overall management and assessment of cases. The social context in which she finds herself can be evaluated through the lenses of key sociological concepts and theories.

Socialisation is one way in which we learn the kind of behaviour that is expected of us in social settings. It is a term and concept used by consensus sociologists when describing the rules that govern thought and behaviour in society. This view claims that social culture exists prior to the people who learn it. In other words, society's cultural rules determine or structure the behaviour of its members. Importantly, the rules are applied not to individuals in a setting, but to the position that they occupy in the structure. Expectations are therefore attached to an individual's position (Jones, 2003). In other positions in other settings, individuals behave differently based on the rules appropriate to the different position, be it as student, daughter or part-time employee. Sociologists call these positions in a social structure 'roles' and the rules regarding their expected behaviour are called 'norms'. There are approved ways of behaving and acting that produce agreed beliefs by members of society, and these contribute to consensus.

In the practice scenario above, Michelle feels that her role as a care worker is undervalued, and she has expressed that she does not feel heard by group members. This may be as a result of Michelle's co-workers viewing her position as less significant or less professionally recognised than other roles. If this is the case, Michelle's contributions and involvement are likely to be less noted or seriously considered. An example of this that Michelle had to learn the 'jargon' of other professionals in order to keep up with discussions at meetings, and also by her reference to a decision-making process that typically ignores her input. With reference, then, to consensus theory, Michelle's role or position may be one that is perceived by others as assisting rather than central to the interdisciplinary work setting and objectives.

Sociologists recognise that people are sometimes constrained not simply by their learned socialisation but also by their unequal position in a particular structure. This is commonly referred to as structural conflict. Unlike consensus sociological theory, conflict theorists argue that rewards and advantages (possessed unequally by different individuals and groups) are the real determinants of behaviour. Repeated tension and arguments amongst staff in the community childcare setting above may indicate that the group is distracted from a central focus on client-centred services. Inherent in this conflict is an imbalance that is likely to escalate due to the advantaged/disadvantaged positions of individuals in the care group. The interdisciplinary group appears to be operating on a basis of influence and short-sighted usefulness, and appears to lack cohesion as well as a set of recognised shared values. In addition, the group is unaware of disproportionate staff involvement (i.e. Michelle's participation) and the consequence of this on their overall service provision.

Sharrock (1977) argues that 'differences of interest are as important to society as agreements upon rules and values ... benefits to a few causes positive discomfort to others' (pp. 515–6). Such inequality is sustainable, however, only when the disadvantaged come to accept their deprivation; that is, when they perceive the inequality as being legitimate. This is done by managing the norms and values of the group. In the above practice scenario, conflict theorists may ask, 'Who benefits from the existing behaviour of group members?' Despite her feelings of protest, Michelle acknowledges her devalued role and has begun to rationalise reasons for her professional marginalisation. She observes 'team alliances' and perceives her relationship to Carol and other colleagues as provisional, based on her agreement with their views. Such feelings may contribute to Michelle's passive acceptance and lack of professional influence.

This outlook is also linked with a third sociological perspective, one referred to as 'interpretive' or 'action theory'. Action theory sees the most important influence on an individual's behaviour as the way that one understands and interacts with others on a micro rather than a macro societal level. Action theory sees an individual's desires and beliefs as meaningful and leading to rational behaviour and relationships. Human action is voluntary and intentional, behaviour that is chosen in order to arrive at a goal, and negotiated interaction with others based on an interpretation of reality. In Michelle's case, the workplace conflict may be a result of misunderstanding or an inability for various professionals to collaborate as equal peers, valuing one another's knowledge and skill contribution to the care service. During meetings, professional boundaries have either not been established or have been breached. Michelle is seen as a 'junior' partner not because of her time interacting with the service-users, but because her role as a social care practitioner is not assessed by her colleagues to be of equal value as other contributing professionals. In today's knowledge economy, a worker such as Michelle should be valued because she can form opinions and apply information in an innovative and creative way. Her knowledge and skills can help to design and develop assistance and a better service outcome for service-users. Social care practitioners are academically and professionally trained and qualified to work as part of a team as well as to work independently. They know how to take initiative and to approach problems with resourceful solutions.

In a team situation, Michelle and her colleagues are defined by a set of group responsibilities focused upon various service-users. They are expected to work together, blending their individual strengths to facilitate a collaborative approach to service provision. McWilliams (2006) identified the challenges of professional co-operation and summarises individual, professional and structural barriers, citing 'a lack of information and understanding amongst professionals of each other's roles, and prejudice amongst the various practitioners is not infrequent' (p. 243). With specific reference to child protection, *Children First* (Department of Health and Children, 1999) emphasises mutual trust amongst professionals as well as an agreement and focus on common goals. Seden (2003) explains how care services vary based on the organisational culture and environment. She describes organisational partnership as having beneficial outcomes (i.e. services) but not without tensions and problems that develop from different ways of working. Similarly, Hardy et al. (1992) summarise barriers to inter-organisational co-ordination as being structurally-, procedurally-, financially-, professionally- and status-based. In response to these increasing challenges, Martin and Henderson (2001) suggest advance planning and identification as ways of building bridges towards an effective partnership and James (1994) views an 'image of connectedness' as a method of defusing conflict and competitiveness. Looking at Michelle's situation, one could regard the different professional roles as complementary rather than competitive, and harmonious rather than incompatible. If left unchecked, however, Michelle's contribution in the above practice scenario will result in a loss of innovative problem-solving and productive service contributions for vulnerable children.

Sociological issues highlighted in this practice scenario include: peer collaboration, workplace conflict, professional boundaries, and professional recognition and responsibility.

PSYCHOLOGICAL PERSPECTIVE

This scenario highlights the tensions that often arise between different professionals working together. The integration of expertise and perspectives of professionals from different disciplines is central to interdisciplinary work (Farhall, 2001). However, intra- and inter-professional rivalries can undermine this work. Such rivalries are characterised by a lack of mutual understanding, competing priorities, status and 'rank' clashes, defensive practices surrounding roles and tasks, 'turf wars', as well as conflict over actual and perceived power (Frost et al., 2005). Additional difficulties include feeling that work is not valued, feeling marginalised, and work practices and agendas being at odds with other professionals (ibid.). Irregular working hours, inadequate administrative and recording systems, high staff turnover and poor managerial relationships are known to undermine interdisciplinary collaboration in the field of social care (Buckley, 2000a; 2002; DOHC, 1999).

In the practice scenario described in this chapter, professional differences between team members appear to contribute to dysfunctional team conflict. However, a certain degree of conflict within a team is beneficial. This is termed 'functional conflict' and motivates staff by raising standards via competition, the consideration of opposing views and thinking more creatively to overcome problems (Riggio, 1990). 'Dysfunctional conflict', on the other hand, refers to conflict which undermines the organisation, the work objectives or work progress. In short, team and group dynamics are major fields of interest for researchers and theorists in social psychology.

Michelle feels that she is going unheard and may feel that her profession is not as 'established' or powerful as some of the others represented in the team. Perhaps some of the others on the team still lack a good understanding of Michelle's professional role. Much has also been written already on the challenges faced by professions in the field of social care (Buckley, 2000a; 2002; Corcoran, 1999; Gallagher & O'Toole, 1999; McKenna-McElwee & Brown, 2005).

The difficulties of interdisciplinary child protection work in particular in Ireland have been illuminated by McWilliams (2006). 'There can often be a lack of information and understanding amongst professionals of each other's roles and prejudice amongst the various practitioners is not infrequent. Single-discipline training is seen to contribute to these difficulties as it offers few opportunities to explore other professionals' perspectives and roles' (p. 243). According to McWilliams (2006), flight (withdrawal) or fight (conflict) responses from professionals inhibit true collaboration and innovative practice resulting in an over-reliance on routine procedures. Such an emphasis on routine protocols and procedures often masks conflicts and differences between professionals, undermining optimal interdisciplinary collaboration (Stevenson, 1999). It is also important for Michelle to show a belief in the contribution and value of her own profession if, as a new profession, Social care is to assume increased status. Ultimately, professionals in multidisciplinary teams need to respect each other, understanding each other's roles, and to recognise that no single profession or approach has all the answers (Buckley, 2000b). In this practice scenario it appears that undue pressure is being exerted by some professionals upon others in the team.

In the scenario described it is also questionable whether a true 'team' exists, or whether it is simply a work group. Work groups, which function based on what members do as individuals are often confused with teams. However, teams require both individual and mutual accountability and are more than simply the sum of their parts. As noted by McGarty (2005), 'Every workplace has groups that range from senior management teams, to project teams to functional teams but a title in itself does not necessarily constitute the team' (p. 202). Not all jobs, however, are compatible with teamworking. Indeed, as with any implementation of work and organisation design, teamworking is more appropriate to some settings than others (Mueller, Procter & Buchanan, 2000). For this reason, the social psychological processes of conformity, obedience, compliance and 'ingroup-outgroup' dynamics, as well as social identity, are also worth exploring with respect to this practice scenario.

Teamwork 'involves people working together to produce work of really high quality by pooling their resources and maximising the potential of each individual. It also requires integrating activity in a coordinated and organised way' (Morley et al., 1998, p. 164). Teams need to achieve consensus based on a shared vision and common overall goals, often developed through teamworker training. Strong leadership is paramount for this in multidisciplinary teams (Brown, 2000; Pine et al., 2003). Effective teamwork relies on clearly defined and agreed objectives, roles and responsibilities, an appropriate skills mix so that team members complement each other, fair distribution of workload, supportive relationships, an ability to deal with disagreements, constructive criticism that is not personal in nature, an accurate awareness of performance levels and capabilities and good leadership (Morley et al., 1998). In this practice scenario, there appears to be a lack of effective leadership present, if any at all.

Role and task ambiguity are also visible in this practice scenario. Interdisciplinary work encourages some 'role-blurring' in striving to achieve collective goals but too much role-blurring is counterproductive (Nolan, 1995). Roles are behaviours shown within the limits of a particular job, and are influenced by personality, both in terms of the roles to which a person is drawn and how these roles are enacted (Pervin, 1989). In the past, attention was paid to 'task' and 'maintenance' roles enacted by members of teams. Ideally, teams require a range of skills and thinking styles with members in roles to which they are suited. A team role, according to Belbin (1993), is the tendency to behave, contribute and to interrelate with others in a particular way. He described nine team roles that organically emerge and which are shared amongst team members for the team to perform optimally. A team of six persons is optimal, with each member adopting a few of the nine roles listed in the appendix. People will typically have preferences for fulfilling each role and may avoid some roles if they can (ibid.). While it is not clear which roles are being undertaken by those mentioned in this practice scenario, an understanding of team roles is helpful and these are included in the appendix.

The practice scenario also shows indicators of work-based conflict. Robbins (1974) identified three sources of conflict:

Communication: referring to conflict due to poor lines of communication and the exchange of information.

Structure: conflict due to role ambiguity (uncertainty over what is or is not part of someone's job), task ambiguity (uncertainty over how certain tasks are divided or how they should be performed) and inequity over the reward allocation (cooperative vs. competitive). Conflict over reward allocation is heightened when the task of one individual is dependent upon another. Differentiation, 'the degree to which tasks and work of individuals or groups is divided' (Huczynski & Buchanan, 1991, p. 550) is a prevalent source of conflict in the workplace. Differentiation contributes to the formation of 'cliques' who establish their own norms, values and practices that may clash with those of other groups or individuals. This contributes to discrimination and prejudice in the workplace. In this practice scenario, Michelle appears to be in a clique and afraid to voice a different opinion to them for fear of being disloyal to this clique and risking their censure.

Personal factors: conflict due to personality, value or priority-clashes between team members.

Another source of conflict was identified by Morley et al. (1998): interdependence contributes to conflict, particularly where the work contributions of some is contingent on those of others. This is often due to people's unhappiness about the performance of others (ibid.).

Super-ordinate goals, shared by all groups in a workplace, are a means of lessening the inter-group conflict. Tasks requiring cooperation and an environment that encourages positive contact and equality between groups are other means of reducing such conflict. Compromise is the primary means of reducing conflict. Conflict-handling strategies employed in different conflict situations as described by Thomas (1976) include:

> **Competition**: a win/lose approach where one worker or group is given prominence, used on critical issues where unpopular actions are required.
>
> **Collaboration compromise**: a mutually acceptable outcome and consensus are sought through collaborative problem-solving.
>
> **Avoidance**: withdrawal from the particular conflict situation by ignoring it or the people involved, or by withholding or disguising information to suppress conflict.
>
> **Accommodation**: one person or group suppresses their own views, enabling those of others to be enacted. Greater value is given to maintaining harmony and avoiding conflict over having one's own perspective or contribution acknowledged.

It is important to note though that conflict resolution is inherently dynamic and interactive. It varies according to situations, those involved and how they respond to events.

Øvretveit (1995) identified five methods of multidisciplinary team decision-making:

- **Practitioner only**: decisions made independently.
- **Practitioner after consultation**: decisions made mostly independently with some team consultation.
- **Practitioner following team policy**: decisions which allow for some practitioner latitude depending on whether the policy is prescriptive or generic.
- **Majority vote**: decisions made with the agreement of the majority of the team.
- **Unanimous**: whereby a vetoing power on the decision is given to team members. Qualified majority voting is another version of this, whereby team members can opt out if they have conflicting responsibilities.

Teamwork is also influenced by the level of team development within the group. Tuckman (1965) described team development in four stages: Forming, Storming, Norming and Performing. When people come together, they form some kind of relationship within their group – the **Forming** stage. Exploring the boundaries of the relationship often involves a little conflict to establish roles and hierarchies and to identify team members' strengths and possible weaknesses. This is the **Storming** stage. When members have established boundaries, they are beginning to feel comfortable with each other when their behaviours are **Norming**. Only then does the group really begin **Performing** and become a team that achieves its objectives. When the dynamics change, the group will revert to the start of the model and so experiences forming and storming again. Change in the team dynamics also occurs when tasks or roles within the team change, or when a team achieves goals (ibid.).

Psychology issues highlighted in this practice scenario include: group processes of compliance, conformity, group polarization, social loafing and persuasion.

PROFESSIONAL PERSPECTIVE
The emergence of social care as a distinct professional field in Ireland has gained momentum over the past ten years. Discussion has now focused on what a social care professional is and does as formal registration has gained statutory footing. The challenge for the emerging profession of social care is to define what distinguishes it from other professions offering health and social services, while at the same time learning to engage with these professions through close interdisciplinary work.

> The whole area of social care is complex and varied, and hence there is a wide spectrum of groups who work in the field, for example child care workers, development workers, gardaí, prison officers, welfare officers, pastoral care workers, social workers and clergy and religious.
>
> (McCann, 1995, p. 31)

To this list you could add probation workers, youth and community workers, and public health nurses, as well as teachers and community health workers. The value of having an explicit, unified model of best practice for how different social professionals, such as social workers and social care practitioners, work together in organisations and teams was highlighted by O'Doherty (2005). This should include clearly articulated lines of responsibility and spheres of autonomy for different professionals as well as objective accountability and common standards of professional excellence.

Practice Scenario Five focuses on Michelle, a community childcare worker who is struggling to establish herself as an 'equal' member of a community care interdisciplinary team. We will begin our discussion by looking at what an interdisciplinary team is, and go on to examine elements of the professional social care role that promote contribution to the team as a whole.

A team is usually defined as a group of people working together towards the achievement of an agreed goal. Of course, agreeing the goal is also part of the team's work. In the social care context, the client or service-user is involved in setting the goal or goals. The team involved brings together professionals from various disciplines. As Williams (2002) puts it: 'Members of the team are selected according to their functional relationship to the client' (p. 213). The better the team works together, the more effective it will be in achieving the best outcomes for the service-user. In Michelle's case, it appears that the team is not working as a cohesive unit. This is not uncommon, as all teams go through stages of development. Williams (2002) identifies these stages as Exploration, Focusing, Gelling and Achievement.

When asked to comment on Michelle's situation, a Community Childcare Worker said that it often takes time for professionals from other, more clearly established disciplines to 'get to know what you do or can do'. She also pointed out that in her experience, there is a hierarchy amongst professionals in the decision-making process. What this shows is that an interdisciplinary team needs to be more than simply a collection of individuals.

Figure 2.1 Concentric Circles of Teamwork

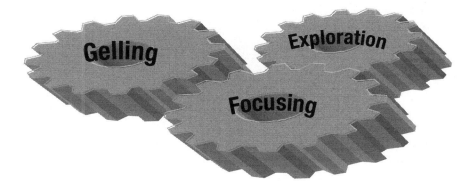

There is no automatic progression through the stages of development identified above. Perhaps it would be more useful to see these stages as interconnected cogs (Figure 2.1 on p. 77). In order to work effectively, team members and leaders must give attention to how they work together.

Michelle seems unsure of herself as a professional within the team. Though she has some allies within the team, she feels undervalued by others. Her strategy, to confront these other team members, may inhibit the team from working together effectively. However, it is important for all team members to get to know each other professionally and understand what each other's perspective can contribute. The Community Childcare Worker we spoke to reported a conscious effort made by her team in building meaningful professional relationships. This effort was facilitated by the team leader, and comprised of developing simple procedures to ensure that each member has a chance to explain the context of their engagement and their current interaction with the service-user. The Community Childcare Worker's advice to Michelle was to 'focus on what she has found out about the situations, what she has experienced, and what she knows'.

A key teamwork skill is assertiveness. Assertiveness has been defined as 'standing up for personal rights and expressing thoughts, feelings and beliefs in direct, honest, and appropriate ways which respect the rights of other people' (Longe & Jakubowski, 1976 in Hargie et al. (1996, p. 269). It is a skill that needs to be learned, developed and practised over time. In order to contribute effectively to the team, each member must be able to communicate clearly from their own perspective. Morrell (1999) contends that professionalism is a result of the interactions of different occupational groups and the extent to which such groups accord each other respect and show cognisance of each other's expertise and role. According to Stuart (2001), social care is distinct from other social professions in that it:

- focuses on relationships with service-users;
- is practised in the milieux or contexts in which the service-users are located;
- has a developmental perspective;
- focuses on social competence rather than illness or pathology; and
- is the team's responsibility to listen to the perspectives, but it is the individual member's responsibility to communicate that perspective.

The challenge for Michelle, as a social care practitioner in our practice scenario, is to balance her own and the team's responsibilities in this regard.

It is worth looking briefly at what leadership means in the context of interdisciplinary work. There are many definitions of leadership, many of which are associated with the qualities assigned to or required by someone in a designated role. Indeed it is true that the interdisciplinary team does need a designated leader to help focus, aid communication and give direction as well as manage change within group membership should this arise. There is another kind of leadership, however, that involves all members of the team. Leadership as an organisational quality emphasises the need to develop a culture that promotes that contribution and potential of individuals. It means giving careful attention to how the group or organisation interacts. Perhaps this is what Michelle is hoping for. In commenting on this practice scenario, the Community Childcare Worker acknowledged that there were institutional and resource issues that often formed bureaucratic blocks to an interdisciplinary team's progress; that professional differences of opinion and internal politics do sometimes inhibit the effectiveness of the team. In spite of these challenges, however, a conscious effort made by the members of the team to focus on client needs and to build an integrated team that values each perspective means that the interdisciplinary team can be more than the sum of its parts.

And finally… The Sainsbury Centre for Mental Health (2001) listed core skills, knowledge and attitudes for multidisciplinary work in the areas of:

- assessment;
- treatment and care management;
- collaborative working;
- management and administration; and
- interpersonal skills.

It may be useful to explore Michelle's role within the multidisciplinary team guided by this list to identify the core skills she needs to develop in order for her to make an effective contribution.

Professional issues highlighted in this practice scenario include:
- **Action Michelle can take to increase her confidence as a care worker on a multi-disciplinary team.**
- **Changes needed in the team to improve the equality of professional roles represented.**
- **Risks to the service-user(s) if team collaboration and professional trust/respect is not facilitated.**

Partnership Approach

Family Resource Centres and their work

There are 100 Family Resource Centres throughout Ireland; each one is different, and responds to the individual needs of the local community. Services provided by FRCs around Ireland include:

- The provision of information, advice and support to target families.
- The provision of education courses and training opportunities.
- The provision of childcare facilities for those attending courses provided by the project.

The aim of Family Resource Centres is to help to combat disadvantage by supporting the functioning of the family unit. Centres provide services for lone parent families, young mothers and others considered in need of extra support. Their approach is based on empowerment, participation and social change.

The Family Support Agency (FSA) was set up as a statutory agency in 2003 to provide support to families, including the provision of core funding and support to Family Resource Centres. This agency also conducts research and advises the Minister for Social and Family Affairs on policy matters affecting families.

Family Resource Centres are supported in their work by Regional Support Agencies and have a national advocacy and networking structure through their representative body, The Family Resource Centre National Forum (FRCNF).

In 1998, the government launched Springboard, an initiative of 15 family support projects. All Springboard projects share a general strategy of being open and available to all families, parents and children in their communities as well as the more specific strategy of working intensively with those who are most vulnerable.

Practice Scenario 6

Setting: Family Resource Centre

Caoimhe works in family support in a Family Resource Centre in a disadvantaged area. Tracey, a lone parent, has begun to come to the centre for help. She is finding it hard to manage financially and is unsure how to cope with her three-year-old son, Aaron, whose behaviour is difficult to control. Tracey also has a five-year-old daughter, Sindy, a lively and energetic child, just beginning junior infants in the local primary school. The children have different fathers.

Tracey is regularly in conflict with members of her family and does not see eye-to-eye with her parents or her older sister. She avoids contact with her immediate family, but does meet up with one of her aunts occasionally. Aaron's father lived with Tracey and the children until Aaron was one, but now comes and goes from their lives. The one time that Caoimhe met him with Tracey on the street she felt a little intimidated and ill-at-ease because he appeared rough and aggressive. He was covered with tattoos and had a nasty-looking dog on a lead. Sindy's father, Mick, is in prison and has little contact with Tracey or Sindy. Mick's mother meets Tracey occasionally and offers food and money every now and then. She has told Tracey that if Mick wasn't in prison he would be fulfilling his responsibilities as a husband and father. Even with occasional support, Tracey feels that Mick's mother disapproves of her ever since she had Aaron, and looks down on her skills as a mother. Both women keep their distance from each other.

As a family support worker, Caoimhe wants to build up a supportive relationship with Tracey so she can help to support her in her parenting. Caoimhe feels, however, that Tracey doesn't take her as seriously as she does other staff in the centre and she wonders if it is because she is younger than Tracey. Recently, Tracey said to her, 'You can't be of any help sure you're just out of college and you don't have any kids yourself.' Caoimhe's supervisor has encouraged her to let Tracey take the lead in terms of directing her where she needs help, adopting a collaborative or 'partnership' approach in her work practice. Caoimhe worries that Tracey's prejudice against her will hinder any productive work between them. She considers asking her line manager if one of the older members of the team might work with Tracey instead.

For further consideration...

- What is my understanding of the term 'family'?
- How do personal values impact on social care professional relationships?
- What is a specific action that Caoimhe can take to increase Tracey's confidence in their working relationship?
- Is it possible that family support would benefit Tracey's extended family? If so, how might a social care practitioner go about facilitating this?

SOCIOLOGICAL PERSPECTIVE

The roles of individuals in modern families are varied and changing. Motherhood, fatherhood, childhood (as well as members of the extended family) are continually being defined and redefined. For example, in Ireland, the political and social contract between women and motherhood is identified in Article 41.2.1 and Article 41.2.2 of the constitution, where women are given primacy by their role as mothers in the home (*Bunreacht na hÉireann*, 1937). At the same time, fathers are missing within this reference, and their role in the family is therefore implied as being outside the home (i.e. earning and providing financially for family members). Several recent factors, however, influence a change in family profiling. One such change is the move of mothers from full-time homemakers to paid employment, either full-time or part-time. This has altered the traditional male 'breadwinner' role to reveal that breadwinning and care giving can be effectively combined. This change has not been without challenges, as both women and men renegotiate their work and family responsibilities. McKeown et al. (1998) argue that as family structures have changed, the status of children within families has risen, giving fathers a greater responsibility and opportunity for caring. Consequently, the role of male breadwinner no longer carries the esteem it once did.

Another change in the family is the rise in one-parent families. Some mothers bring up their children without financial support of the children's father, relying instead on their own independent earnings. Other mothers take state welfare payments as a replacement for the traditional male breadwinner's earnings. Either route can leave fathers marginalised or alienated because they are unable or unwilling to contribute to their children's welfare. McKeown et al. (1998) note that 'the severing of parenthood from marriage also serves to crystallise the definition of mother and father as involving a relationship with their child rather than with each other' (p. 27). In the practice scenario above, Tracey has two children by different fathers, neither of whom appear to be significantly involved in their child's life. Either by choice or circumstances, Tracey has been left to care for her children as a single parent. Although she would benefit from support from her extended family, as would her children, she finds the regular conflict difficult and chooses instead to seek support from social services. Research conducted by Corcoran (2005) found that the majority of young, unemployed or poorly paid, poorly educated fathers reported feelings of anger and fear in their role as fathers. Many also stated that their attempts to co-parent were undermined by the child's mother, who was perceived to have control in the relationship (pp. 142–3). Interestingly, research conducted by McKeown and colleagues (2003) found that there was no significant variation in children's well-being based on family type. Rather than parents' marital status or even the presence of one or two parents in the household, well-being for children from lone-parent families was first based on the child's perception of unresolved conflict in the family, followed secondly by a supportive mother who was able to resolve conflict with her partner. The third factor was a supportive father and the fourth, a reasonably stable family income. It is worth noting, however, that family type had a significant influence on the psychological well-being of mothers from one-parent families.

Sometimes, people share similar family values but engage in different family practices because they are obliged to fashion their lives under different conditions. This appears to be the situation for Tracey in the practice scenario above. Although she seems to make choices that alienate the fathers of her children and their families (as well as her own), this has developed out of circumstances that were most likely unplanned or unintended. When family change occurs in this manner, sociologists refer to it as 'situational diversity' (see, for example, Cheal, 2002). Although cultural ideals of the family continue to be supported by the majority of the population and by major social institutions both religious and political, situational diversity occurs when people spend most or part of their lives in alternative living arrangements. Although we can expect that most people will live in different ways at different times in their lives, some changes are often unsolicited. For example, Tracey lived in a nuclear family during her childhood (i.e. with parents and a sibling), but she now finds herself living in a family situation without the regular presence of a husband/father, or regular support from an extended family network.

Talcott Parsons (1971), a functionalist sociologist, theorised that the nuclear family was least stable among people who had low incomes and low education. He maintained that the struggles to make ends meet caused family disorganisation and, often, family breakdown. Parsons is criticised by research that found compensatory strength in extended family networks as well as later trends of separation and divorce in middle-class society. Parsons' views were corroborated by Murray (1984) who claimed that state welfare reforms undermined the family by providing disincentives to traditional marriage.

In contrast, many sociologists view changes in family patterns as resulting from socio-economic stratification in which those in the lower classes have fewer opportunities for education and employment and a decline in community norms (see, for example, Blaikie, 1996; Wilson, 1987, 1996 and Cheal, 2002). When this occurs, disadvantaged individuals may fail to engage with systems or institutions that would otherwise support their social and/or economic needs. In their small-scale study of vulnerable fathers, Ferguson and Hogan (2004) sought to develop a 'father-inclusive framework' for family policy and practice. They found a practice of 'father exclusion' by social service providers. In some cases this was due to fathers' appearance (e.g. tattoos, scars, piercings) that stereotyped them as unfit to care for children. The research concluded that social workers have little confidence in such fathers and lacked the skills to engage in meaningful discussions with them. Research by Buckley (1998) and McKeown (2001) confirms this bias, pointing out that the role of the father in family cases is filtered out or even rendered invisible within the family support system.

An additional factor in the changing family profile is the shift from an emphasis on getting married to an emphasis on having a meaningful relationship. Giddens (1992) argues that social expectations make some people less inclined to marry. Instead, they seek relationships that will provide personal satisfaction and fulfilment rather than social conformity, resulting in a challenge to cultural traditions and religious customs. Consequently, some people enter into new relationships several times in their lives, leading to family forms that are increasingly complex and diverse. Individuals like Tracey may be more affected by social policies that view lone parents as 'social problems' or as a threat to the social order or family values. Single parents often have difficulty balancing the demands of family life and paid employment and support from social services may help to provide assistance that would otherwise come from family members or private service providers. Because of the demand on limited social resources, contemporary welfare services are attempting to establish more partnerships between service-users, pre-existing networks (i.e. extended family, friends) and public services. Caoimhe is in a position to act as a catalyst for these provisions. A large-scale study conducted by Bebbington and Miles (1989) in the *British Journal of Social Work* found that white children from two-parent families with three or fewer children living in an owner-occupied house had a one in 7,000 chance of entering care. A child from a large, one-parent family living on income support, of mixed ethnic origin, and living in rented accommodation had a one in ten chance of entering care. Their conclusions were not that poor children go into care, but rather that social deprivation and exclusion makes parenting much harder.

In its attempt to establish a meaningful role for families and the larger community in the lives of Irish children, the Department of Health and Children published a document entitled *The Agenda for Children's Services: A Policy Handbook* (DOHC, 2007). It proposes a framework for establishing accessible, effective and sustainable services for all children and their families and stresses the point that 'social care services for children do not exist as an alternative to the care and concern that generally only families and communities can provide in a sustained and effective manner' (p. 23). Applying this framework to the practice scenario above, Caoimhe is in a position to offer her support services in a way that will identify, understand and optimise the strengths within the informal networks (i.e. extended family and community) of which Tracey and her children are a part. *The Agenda for Children's Services* highlights the importance of explicit and active commitment towards utilising family, friends and community in working with children (p. 18). Caoimhe has a mandate, as a service-provider to facilitate a shared approach to developing services in a way that will maximise the desired outcome for Tracey and her family. *The Agenda for Children's Services* emphasises the following principles of action towards developing services:

- Working in partnership with children, families, professionals and communities.
- Needs-led and striving for the minimum intervention required.
- Clear focus on the wishes, feelings, safety and well-being of children.
- Reflects a strengths-based/resilience perspective.
- Strengthens informal support networks.
- Accessible and flexible, incorporating both child protection and out-of-home care.
- Facilitates self-referral and multi-access referral paths.
- Involves service-users and front-line providers in the planning, delivery and evaluation of services.
- Promotes social inclusion, addressing issues of ethnicity, disability and rural/urban communities.
- Measures of success are routinely built into provision so as to facilitate evaluation.

(p. 35)

From the moment we are born, we are social beings who spend most of our lives in some form of social grouping. Despite the changes family groups make, we participate in and have connections to other social groups that affect our lives, relationships and sense of well-being. Caoimhe, in partnership with Tracey, her family and other professional service-providers can negotiate required procedures and practices in order to achieve full participation and cooperation in meeting the needs of each participant.

Sociological issues highlighted in this practice scenario include:
- Defining 'the family' and its place in society.
- Social stratification, marginalisation and exclusion.
- Social roles and family support work.

PSYCHOLOGICAL PERSPECTIVE

Psychology, as a discipline, offers much to help us understand how we relate to others, respecting people as individuals with due regard to their rights. How relationships are formed, develop and are maintained, as well as how good working collaborative relationships are forged, are popular fields of investigation for psychological research. The importance given by Caoimhe's line manager to developing a 'working partnership' with service-users, such as Tracey, and the need for Caoimhe to develop a relationship with Tracey to achieve this, are both issues to which psychology has much to contribute.

The professional–parent relationship or 'partnership with parents or service-users' has been accorded ever-increasing importance across the spectrum of social care work (Buckley, 2002; Pelchat & Lefebvre, 2004; Sloper, 1999) In order to empower families, paternalistic working practices need to be set aside in favour of a partnership-based approach. Partnership reflects the belief that parents and professionals are 'capable individuals who become more capable by sharing knowledge, skills and resources' (Dunst et al., 1988, p. 9). However, what actually constitutes 'partnership' in the context of social care work? For some theorists it simply means parental participation in processes with professionals. It requires a range of relationship, advocacy, negotiation and organisational skills. Partners need to find the right balance between flexibility and accountability, which is difficult to achieve given the power imbalance and complex organisational factors that may affect the work of the partnership (Balloch & Taylor, 2001).

According to Lee (1999), partnership involves qualities such as negotiation and equality. However, is there ever true equality as the balance of power often shifts between people (McIntosh & Runciman, 2008)?

Bimead and Crowley (2005) described eleven key features of a partnership:

1. a genuine, trusting relationship;
2. honest and open communication and listening;
3. participation and involvement;
4. support and advocacy;
5. working together with negotiation of goals, plans and boundaries;
6. reciprocity (mutual exchange of information, actions);

7. praise and encouragement;
8. empathy;
9. sharing and respect for each other's expertise;
10. information-giving; and
11. the enabling of choice and equity.

The importance of involving parents in child protection and care is enshrined in *Children First* (DOHC, 1999) and recognises that family members possess unique knowledge about their own and each other's strengths and weaknesses. Springboard projects in Ireland are an example of where a partnership approach can be seen in family support work. The six key strengths identified by past research on these projects are:

1. A general attitude to the family that is strengths-based, non-stigmatising, non-judgemental and grounded in advocacy.
2. A solution-focused, holistic approach to problems that is flexible and realistic.
3. A positive, genuine, sensitive, committed and approachable disposition amongst staff.
4. A partnership approach with the family and other key agencies.
5. A community-based location and orientation, which is accessible, responsive, knowledgeable about the local situation and family histories, and places a premium on being accepted in the community.
6. A facility that is accessible, informal and non-threatening.

(McKeown et al., 2000)

Working in partnership brings with it many challenges. Parents are often concerned about relinquishing their children's care and welfare to another person. They may be fearful about disclosing the 'full picture' of their problems in case it compromises them in seeking help. Professionals may have difficulty in trusting parents in case they are being manipulated by the parents, resulting in the children being at greater risk than initially thought. 'Disguised compliance' (pretence of agreement and acquiescence), a control conflict described by Reder and colleagues (1993) is a particular concern in child protection work. This was highlighted by the statutory inquiry into the Kelly Fitzgerald case in Ireland in the 1990s. Professionals may also not have the training or time to develop such a partnership approach. Additionally, poor inter-professional or inter-agency collaboration, as well as conflicting advice given to a family from different professionals also undermines a professional's ability to undertake a partnership approach with a family (Watson et al., 2002). Professionals can be ambivalent or even highly resistant 'about abandoning a style of work which is power-laden, formal and individualised in favour of an approach which involves greater sharing groups and more negotiated, informal work' (O'Doherty, 2005, pp. 115–6).

It is worth mentioning that the 'partnership approach' itself has been criticised. Issues raised include: an over-concentration on process features (how well are we working together?) rather than on their outcomes (does it make any difference for service-users?); seeing partnership as an end in itself, not as a means to an end; lack of clarity about which forms of partnership are most appropriate in achieving the outcomes sought (Glasby & Dickinson, 2008).

Relationship-building

This practice scenario illuminates the importance of relationship building in social care practice. Psychologists have identified many factors that impair communication and inhibit relationship development. These include a professional's expectations, values, held stereotypes and prejudices, often expressed unconsciously through non-verbal behaviour. Lishman (1994) identified key factors in building and maintaining relationships: warmth, genuineness, acceptance, encouragement and approval, empathy and responsiveness, and sensitivity. These relate to the qualities of congruence, empathy and respect highlighted by Carl Rogers in therapeutic relationships and discussed in the professional perspective in this practice scenario.

In this scenario, Tracey's comment to Caoimhe may have led Caoimhe to withdraw from her and question her own abilities as a professional. It may have triggered latent worries Caoimhe had about working with families, for example, her inexperience in family work and being younger than many of the parents, including Tracey, who attend the centre. In turn, Caoimhe's withdrawal and apparent lack of subsequent interest in Tracey and her children may only serve to make Tracey feel that she was right in the first place regarding Caoimhe's lack of empathy and responsiveness to her situation. She might, perhaps, have misread Caoimhe's behaviour as showing disapproval for her as a mother, or perhaps she felt that Caoimhe was 'acting' the role and not being sufficiently genuine in her approach.

Much has already been written about the use of self in care practice (Elson, 1988; Goldstein, 2001; Garafat, 2005; Ward, 2003, 2008). Kennefick (2006) emphasised the importance of personal and interpersonal development work in social care training as a means of developing interpersonal skills for care practice. 'It is about not only looking but seeing as well, about not only listening but hearing as well and with full emotional support. It is about the embodying of experience' (Kennefick, 2003, p. 92).

This encompasses listening skills, self-awareness, emotion and motive exploration and exploration of the self as a 'meaning-maker'. 'Things or events generally do not have an inherent meaning; people give meaning to them. It follows that each individual gives a different meaning, creates a unique interpretation of each event' (Kennefick, 2006, p. 215). In relating to others professionally, social care practitioners need to be aware of the meanings they ascribe to people and events and the potential personal and professional reasons why they do so.

Role of fathers in family support work

The role of fathers (and the extended family network) in family support is another factor for consideration in relation to our practice scenario. Irish research has reported that social work in general is much less father-inclusive than the work of voluntary agencies like family centres. This is despite the fact that the inclusion of fathers can make statutory obligations to promote children's welfare easier to discharge. When family centres have policies to actively include fathers, such as refusing to accept referrals without reference to the father, men are much more likely to engage.

However, engaging fathers is typically not seen as a matter of human rights. According to Ferguson and Hogan (2004, p. 6):

> The most effective father-inclusive practitioners are those who are able to go beyond the one-dimensional imagery of dangerous masculinity to hold a view of men's identities as multi-layered and complex, and containing resources to care for children as well as possible risks, and to develop those caring capacities accordingly.

A dilemma for professionals, like Caoimhe and her colleagues, is that vulnerable fathers are sometimes construed as dangerous and unfit to care. Involving them in childcare is thus seen as a risk. A 're-framing' of practice is thus needed to view fathers more as an 'untapped resource' for the child's welfare and development as opposed to being considered a risk. Research suggests 'that this is not simply a matter of what gets done by single agencies or professionals working alone but emphasises the centrality of inter-agency perspectives (and tensions) in how father's identities are constructed (ibid., p. 12). However, a father may not be willing to engage even if the mother wishes them to. The same research by Ferguson and Hogan (2004) on the fears men have of involvement with professionals in the care of their children identified:

- Going against a definition of masculinity which values strength and coping, and repudiates vulnerability and needing support.
- Being seen with children at all due to a past history of violence, and so trying to keep a low profile – to 'be there' without being noticed.
- Being discovered defrauding social security.

Agencies, such as family resource centres, can encourage greater father involvement by having a father-inclusive framework. This involves:

- Clear father-inclusive policies.
- An ethos that challenges stereotypical assumptions about masculinity and gender roles by working through the staff members' 'macho fixations' and images of 'dangerous' masculinity.
- Practical skills and techniques to engage men and 'hold' them in the family work.
- A belief that men can nurture and develop as carers, that they matter in the care of their children.

Another key issue that needs to be tackled in being 'father-inclusive' is what Morrell (1999) termed 'inscrutable masculinity': the paradox that men resist getting help, especially at times of crisis when they most need it. 'Help-seeking' was being resisted because it goes against a man's self-image and is seen as a threat to status or image that would only add to their problems (Ferguson & Hogan, 2004).

The work of Caoimhe and her colleagues in assisting service-users like Tracey and her family cannot be underestimated. Family support projects in Ireland, such as the Springboard project, have been extremely successful in helping vulnerable families and children at risk and have had added benefits at the community level (McKeown et al., 2001). Colm O'Doherty's (2007) book *A New Agenda for Family Support: Providing services that create social capital* provides a very useful discussion on the role of family support in harnessing and enhancing social capital in contemporary Ireland.

Psychological issues highlighted in this practice scenario include:
- **Understanding the dynamics of the professional relationship.**
- **The 'self' in social care practice.**
- **Including fathers – overcoming barriers.**
- **Prejudice and the field of social cognition, personality and 'personality clashes' as well as parenting (explored later in Practice Scenario Nine).**

PROFESSIONAL PERSPECTIVE

One of the defining features of social care work is that it is relationship-based. The relationship that exists between worker and service-user creates the space in which positive outcomes can be achieved. This discussion will centre on partnership as an approach to establishing and maintaining that working relationship. Partnership suggests that the working relationship is characterised by 'doing with' rather than 'doing for'. This approach demands of the social care worker empathy, genuineness, objectivity and self-awareness. (In care practice, 'the self' is an instrument to help the other person(s).) This is important in addressing values, both personal and professional; how past experiences have shaped one's own development and how one relates to others and construes situations. It involves being cognisant of feelings and reactions experienced in responding to others and to the situations encountered. All of these can influence a professional's behaviour and relationships with others and so require consideration. These professional demands challenge the social care worker particularly those new to practice like Caoimhe. In coming to terms with a complex and sometimes reluctant service-user, she gets to know herself not only as a professional but as a person. By using supervision Caoimhe can explore her developing personal and professional self.

We will now take a closer look at three key elements of relationship-building.

Empathy

Defined as 'the accurate understanding of the feelings of a client but not sharing those feelings' (O'Farrell, 1999). To achieve this 'accurate understanding', the worker must create a space in which the service-user is secure and feels safe. An experienced Family Support worker we spoke to summed up the approach as follows: 'Time is needed. Caoimhe needs time to allow the family to get to know her, to build up the relationship.' So, while the issues that Tracey and her family face may be obvious, time needs to be given to establish a trusting relationship that will allow them to be tackled using a partnership approach. Caoimhe must try to convey that she understands what Tracey is feeling; a starting point might be to work with Tracey to name those feelings.

Genuineness

'The simplest way of thinking about genuineness is to regard it as open communication' (Murgatroyd, 1996, p. 3). This aspect of professional social care or 'helping' work generally raises a key question for the worker: How much of 'themselves' do they bring to the helping relationship? For example, in our practice scenario Tracey challenges Caoimhe's professional competence by saying, 'You can't be of any help. Sure you are just out of college and you don't have any kids yourself.' Rather than seeing this comment as a threat or an attempt to undermine her professional role, Caoimhe may view it as a genuine attempt by Tracey to test the relationship – to test the genuineness of the person she is being asked to trust. If Caoimhe communicates openly at this stage, she can help to build that trust. The experienced professional we spoke to encouraged an immediate and open response, too: 'I'd respond immediately … I'd acknowledge it, say, 'Yes, I worked hard and got some knowledge that might help here … let's give it a try for a while and we'll see then.' The attempt at open communication here is more important than the actual words used. It models for the service-user a way of developing a working partnership that forms the basis for future work.

Objectivity

As a social care skill, objectivity is the developed ability to separate one's own feelings from situations presented by a service-user. If a working partnership is to be achieved each party in that partnership must feel empowered and valued as a person with a recognised right to make their own choices and decisions. Once again, the professional relationship between worker and service-user, helper and helped comes into focus. Once again, the importance of recognising that it is ultimately a relationship between person and person, each bringing their unique perspective must be faced. We have already seen that empathy can help to establish the foundation of a trusting relationship. Neil Thompson in his book, *People Skills*, emphasises the value of interpersonal interactions in professional care work: 'It is often through interpersonal interactions that change takes place, that problems are solved and quality of life improved' (2002, p. 73). There is a professional responsibility for the social care worker to bring objectivity to these interactions. According to Miley and colleagues (2004, p. 56), 'honest feedback which describes rather that evaluates a client's behaviour reflects objectivity'.

Objectivity, genuineness and empathy are key building blocks of the professional social care working relationship. They help to establish and maintain the space in which positive change can be achieved by the service-user in partnership with the worker. However, what has become clear in our brief discussion of Caoimhe's work scenario is that these are not simply learned skills that, once mastered, can be produced on demand to achieve a predictable outcome. On the contrary; social care work is often characterised by longer-term working relationships between service-user and worker, with each relationship developing in its own unique way, being explored, tested, rejected and embraced. The ability of the worker to work with this level of closeness to service-users whilst maintaining a professional perspective is a difficult balancing act, one that demands that they keep in touch with their own personal-development journey. This is why supervision needs to be seen as an integral part of social care work, not just by the individual worker but by the service-providing organisation as a whole. 'A working environment which helps workers to explore issues relating to their role is likely to produce workers who help service-users explore issues relating to the workers role – leading in turn to more effective work.' (Trotter, 1999, p. 58).

Practice Scenario Six saw Caoimhe worry about how her role was viewed by the young woman with whom she was working. Supervision is provided and may help Caoimhe to explore her own feelings about work in a safe environment allowing her to stay with the developing working relationship with her service-user. O'Neill (2004) defines professional supervision as 'a partnership process between the supervisor, supervisee and the organisation', one that 'provides a regular, structured opportunity to discuss work, to reflect on practice and progress and to plan for future development'. Without supervision, it is less likely that the relationship between worker and service-user will reach a level of partnership needed for progress to be made. As Thompson (2002, p. 57) puts it: 'Effective supervision can be the difference between: success and failure; stress and satisfaction; worry and reassurance; good practice and excellent practice.'

Professional issues highlighted in this practice scenario include:
- **The skills behind relationship-building.**
- **Self-awareness and professional development.**
- **Values in the social care workplace.**

PART THREE

ETHICS

Ethics: History and Applications

Ethics is derived from the Greek word '*ethikos*' meaning disposition. At its most fundamental level, ethics is concerned with the study of whether a decision/action is right or wrong as well as the goodness and badness of motives and actions.

Professional ethics in social care is concerned with core values, moral principles and their application in care practice. How professionals relate to service-users, confidentiality, accountability, reporting of malpractice and professional integrity are key considerations in social care ethics. More specifically, social care ethics involves attention to empathy, equality, sensitivity and respect in a professional's relationships with service-users. Maintenance of professional and personal boundaries, balancing professional responsibilities with service-user rights, and working with conflict are other areas of ethical concern for the social care professional, as are empowerment, advocacy, anti-oppressive practice and social justice – topics which also feature prominently in sociology, social policy and law.

Professional ethics in social care also requires attention to a professional's care of self and their understanding of their own values, feelings and reasoning about decisions and actions taken in practice. As noted by the philosopher Socrates in Ancient Greece, optimal care for others requires a developed sense of care of oneself. These ethical topics are also discussed in depth by Charleton (2007) and Banks (2006).

In any profession, European and national legislation as well as professional and agency 'codes of practice' guide professional practice. At a legislative level, the Republic of Ireland has ratified the United Nations International Covenants on Economic, Social and Cultural Rights and on Civil and Political Rights, as well as the United Nations Convention on the Rights of the Child and various other international and European human rights instruments. In 2001, the Council of Europe ratified a recommendation asking member states to support the development of codes of ethics in line with existing international instruments and requiring agencies to promote good practice through the integration of ethical codes in services. National legislation such as *Children First* and policies such as our 'duty to care', inform ethical practice in social care as do national standards such as the 'National Standards for Children's Residential Centres' published by the Department of Health and Children (DOHC), and the National Standards for Disability Services currently being developed by the National Disability Authority (www.nda.ie). However, codes of practice/ethics are not without their limitations. Codes are seen by some as based on transient laws and societal attitudes (Gillon, 1992) and, as noted by O'Hagan and Dillenberger (1995, p. 15):

> Sometimes the principles enunciated by such codes can be so general and platitudinous that they offer little in terms of (1) understanding the problem to which they may be applied and (2) guiding childcare workers through the ethical minefields which many childcare dilemmas constitute.

Codes of practice, along with a professional's own moral conscience, do serve, however, as points of reference for a professional when considering the ethical dimensions of any work situation. Infringement of codes of practice or legislation may lead a professional to being 'struck off' a register of such professionals, where this exists. In Ireland, this register is in the process of development for social care practitioners and others working in the health and care fields. This will make it a 'statutory' profession, a self-regulating profession with supervisory and disciplinary powers, backed up by legislation. Statutory professional bodies can set rules and standards binding for all practitioners of the profession, demand accountability and exercise discipline on those who transgress such rules (Mills, 2002). Non-statutory professions may have an overarching body, but this does not have any power to regulate the profession as described above. While trying to ensure the best care of service-users, professional codes also serve to safeguard the profession itself by determining what values are in the best interests of the profession and through setting nationwide standards of training, conduct and competence (ibid.). Professional codes also help to illuminate what, in the eyes of the profession, may constitute professional misconduct, such as dishonourable behaviour where there is some component of moral failure as well as persistent negligence or recklessness (ibid.). The Irish Association for social care workers (www.iascw.ie)

stipulates that the social care worker must contribute to the physical, intellectual, emotional, social and moral welfare of service-users in a context in which every effort is made to ensure that the nature and purpose of any care and treatment given is understood by the service-user. The social care worker must:

- respect each person as an individual by ensuring that the dignity, privacy and rights of service-users are safeguarded;
- be honest, trustworthy, reliable and dependable while giving precedence to professional responsibility over personal interest in the discharge of duty;
- arrive for duty in a fit state mentally and physically;
- respect the rights of service-users while ensuring, in as far as possible, that their actions or behaviour do not harm themselves or others;
- always promote the best interests of service-users by following established policies and procedures to challenge and report behaviour or practices, which are abusive, dangerous, discriminatory or exploitative;
- make known to service-users in a clear, understandable and unequivocal manner the process of making a complaint in respect of service provision or abuse;
- ensure that accurate, objective and confidential records are kept in respect of service-users;
- recognise and accept that information received in a professional capacity should not be used for other purposes;
- understand and accept that exemption from professional confidentiality can only be justified in terms of higher priority in the interests of the service-user or in a court of law; and
- uphold the dignity of the social care profession and do not engage in any activity, personally or socially, which may bring the profession into disrepute.

(ibid.)

In the field of disability, many organisations have, or are in the process of developing, their own code of practice or 'statement of ethos'. For students on professional practice placements, the Irish Association of Social Care Education (IASCE) Statement of Principles provides an ethical code of practice. Ethics is also covered in social care training, delivered as distinct modules or within professional development/practice modules. Emphasis is given in such modules to encouraging students to become aware of and reflect on ethical issues, considering competing arguments, examining the strengths and limitations of opposing arguments and reaching reasoned decisions.

In the UK, Berry (cited in Sale, 2002), contends that such codes are important for all involved in social care, setting down and establishing practice and conduct for social care workers and employers. These inform social care workers what is expected of them and also clarify for service-users what to expect from social care workers. These act as a publicly acknowledged set of standards to which social care workers are publicly accountable. According to Watkins (cited in Sale, 2002), in the UK, codes of conduct present a nice image of social care, but the reality is harsher. Watkins advocates a more balanced account of the work social care staff do be reflected in the codes, complete with guidance on how staff can achieve their requirements, including examples about how to do care tasks.

Codes and standards help to clarify professional responsibilities and protect against institutional abuse. Institutional abuse includes physical, emotional and sexual abuse or neglect by an individual staff member as well as programme abuse and system abuse. Programme abuse occurs when programmes within institutions fall below accepted standards or rely on harsh or inhumane techniques to modify behaviour. System abuse, on the other hand, refers to 'any system, programme, policy procedure or individual interaction with a child in placement that abuses, neglects or is detrimental to the child's well-being (Gil in Department of Health, 1996, p. 30). System abuse is not carried out by any single person or programme, but arises as a consequence of the care system being inadequate, 'stretched beyond its limits and incapable of guaranteeing safety to all children in care' (Gil, 1982, p. 8). The 'Report on the Inquiry into the Operation of Madonna House' (Department of Health, 1996) drew attention to this in respect to residential childcare in Ireland. Factors, such as inadequate complaints procedures, the closed nature of some institutions (where internal criticism and complaints are stifled), the dynamics of power in care services and other barriers to the disclosure and reporting of abuse, were highlighted in this report. In another statutory report, 'Interim Report of the Joint Committee on the Family' (Department of Health, 1996), shortcomings in health and social work involvement, with a case of child neglect in a family in the community, were identified, illustrating practices falling below standards necessary for the adequate care and protection of vulnerable children. This report identified that 'boundaries between personal needs and professional roles had become confused, possibly leading to the worker becoming over-involved and over-identified with the family' (ibid., p. 183).

With particular reference to residential childcare, Craig and colleagues (1998) elaborated on eight key principles that should guide professionals in their work. These are: respecting and facilitating the individuality and development of children; respecting and facilitating children's rights and responsibilities; ensuring good basic care; support and encouragement of children in their education; identifying and meeting children's health needs; working in partnership with parents, whenever in the best interests of the child; multidisciplinary work that shows child-centred collaboration; and enabling children to feel safe and secure in care. These principles are also worth deliberating, with respect to the scenarios presented in this section.

Across the three practice scenarios presented in this theme, a number of common ethical issues can be found. These include: balancing personal and professional boundaries and values, confidentiality, the use (and abuse) of power and non-judgemental practice. These are fundamental concerns for professional practice across the care sector. Specific sociological, psychological and professional practice concepts are also discussed in relation to the scenarios illustrating the application of theory to practice. The views of service-providers and service-users are also drawn upon in the professional perspective, providing views from the 'coal face' on the issues raised in each scenario. It is also worthwhile considering the practice scenarios bearing in mind the IASCW code of practice outlined above.

– 7 –

Personal and Professional Boundaries

- Cannabis, opiates and cocaine are the main problem drugs (other than alcohol) reported by people seeking treatment for the first time in Ireland. Numbers reporting cocaine have increased significantly over recent years.
- Nearly one fifth of new cases presenting for treatment are under 18 years of age.
- Drug misuse is a nationwide concern and is not exclusively a Dublin-based problem.
- In 2006, 5,191 people sought treatment for problem drug use. Over half of these received counselling, two-fifths received methadone treatment, one fifth received a brief intervention and one in seven attended medication-free therapy.
- Poly-drug use and the increasing number of people with a non-Irish nationality are current considerations in treatment services (Reynolds et al., 2008).

Practice Scenario 7

Setting: Addiction Support Service

An agency runs support groups for parents of recovering drug addicts. These groups are co-facilitated by experienced staff members. Parents share stories and struggles, wins and losses in the ongoing battle of coping with the effects of drug misuse by a family member. These shared stories often go far beyond everyday life experiences to include discussion of past family turmoil, significant events and relationships within and outside the family. Sometimes facilitators can feel angry, sad or overwhelmed by what is said. They often feel humbled by the courage and resilience of the group participants. The task of the facilitators is to encourage and guide the group safely through the meetings.

One of the facilitators, Karen, relates particularly well to one of the parents, Owen, who reminds her of her brother Tom who lives in Australia. She'd like to invite Owen and his wife Sheila around to her house sometime to meet her husband Declan, especially because Owen is an avid snooker player, like Declan. While Karen gets on well with the other facilitators, she hasn't forged any strong friendships with her colleagues there.

A question asked recently at the end of a meeting struck Karen: 'Ye know an awful lot about us, but how come we know nothing about ye?' Karen is particularly cautious about revealing too much about herself, as she views herself first and foremost as a facilitator. However, she recognises that the reason she is reluctant to develop close friendships with colleagues is because they may uncover what she feels is a less-than-privileged background. Unlike most of her colleagues, Karen was isolated from her community as a child because her father was long-term unemployed and her mother suffered from depression. Left to mind themselves, Karen and her brother kept each other company throughout their childhood years, rarely socialising with others outside the family. As a result, Karen grew up feeling insignificant and marginalised. Karen's job as a facilitator has been her first opportunity to experience a sense of status and prestige. She identifies with the parents in the group, yet feels proud of herself because she has overcome her social obstacles.

For further consideration...

1. As a starting point for understanding yourself as a professional, explore your own motivation to become a social care professional.
2. What makes you relate better to some people rather than to others, in terms of personality features, background, interests and values?
3. How should Karen's supervisor and team colleagues respond if Karen told them about her this situation?
4. What is professional judgement? It has been said that it is judgement that comes from experience, that is, experience that comes from bad judgement. What have you learned from the decisions, both good and bad, that you have made in care practice? Consider what you have learned from mistakes made in care practice (Davis, 1992).
5. What is an example of reflective work that might support Karen at a personal and professional level?
6. What alternative actions can Karen implement to affirm her professional role in the support group?
7. What sociological concepts support a healthy and appropriate service-user/service-provider relationship?

SOCIOLOGICAL PERSPECTIVE

In the above scenario, Karen is proud of her personal and professional qualification as a social care worker and has a sense of status and prestige as a facilitator in the drug rehabilitation centre. Sociologists describe status as a social honour given to an individual or group in society. It is often associated with social positions of power or advantage and is recognised by particular styles or symbols, such as language, apparel or occupation. Status can help to shape an individual's social standing or can distinguish him or her from other individuals or groups in a community. Although status can sometimes be associated with an individual's social class (i.e. economic wealth or income), it is often a result of social categorisation, such as ethnicity, ability, age, or gender. In Karen's case, she has experienced social mobility as she has moved up the social scale as a result of her professional qualification and working life. Sociologists often measure an individual's social mobility by comparing their social movement, position and hierarchy to that of their parents. Karen tells herself that she has overcome the social obstacles associated with her upbringing and background, yet she still feels socially marginalised from her work colleagues and is allowing herself to become emotionally aligned with a service-user as a result.

Social and professional boundaries

Karen is to be commended for her sympathetic and insightful approach to Owen. As a facilitator in a support group for parents of drug addicts, she is aware of the vulnerable situation of many parents. She is also trained to recognise her own place (i.e. emotionally) and professional role in the support group. Understandably, Karen will find that she has more in common with some parents than with others, yet her relationship with all group members must remain appropriate. There are many codes of professional conduct associated with social service providers, and most call for the establishment and maintenance of appropriate boundaries between care providers and service-users. (For a useful example of a policy document on personal and professional boundaries see 'Policy for Personal and Professional Boundaries' NHS, 2007). While respecting the needs and rights of the parents in the support group, Karen has begun to cross a crucial boundary line by considering social contact with Owen and his wife outside of the formal social service setting – in this case, the support group meeting. While it is agreed that care workers should establish a good rapport with service-users, it should always be done with a focus on meeting the needs of the service-user rather than one's own needs. Karen's plan could make Owen dependent on her, and even on her husband by encouraging an unwarranted shift of focus from the needs of Owen to the needs of Karen. This is likely if Karen moves the professional relationship towards one of friendship.

Ignoring established conventions that help to maintain a necessary professional distance between service-users and service-providers can lead to boundary violations. The scenario above provides a good example of this when Karen considers meeting Owen in a social setting rather than in their professional setting. This blurring of boundaries can confuse Owen with respect to Karen's role in the support group regarding any expectation of friendship. In her training for social care, Karen learned about the power relationships that exist between service-provider and service-user and of the importance of self-reflective practice. She has been taught to recognise hazardous practices in her work that compromise her professionalism and effectiveness. In the scenario above, Karen should ensure that all interaction with Owen remains within the context of their professional relationship and in an appropriate setting.

Social roles

Part of Karen's social care training stressed the importance of ongoing professional development. A dual-focus approach in her personal development emphasises a focus on the actual work to be done (i.e. the task) as well as a focus on the care practitioner doing that work (Kennefick, 2006; O'Neill, 2003). This approach looks at the impact of the work being done, as well as the impact of person doing the work. In other words, the connection between the care provider and the service-user and the mutual communication that results in their relationship determines the effectiveness of the professional effort. Sociology teaches us that each society has a process of socialising its members. It emphasises one's social roles and highlights the process of learning what is appropriate behaviour in a given social situation (e.g. at work, in the family, etc.). Through socialisation, each of us is taught certain ways of behaving and relating to each other. Our identity is formed by our social relationships with others and is variable (e.g. multiple roles, such as care worker, neighbour, daughter, sister, parent) depending on our social encounters. It is not uncommon, however, that society's demands on our lives cause us to limit our personal growth or representation. When this occurs, an individual may unknowingly use other people to satisfy underlying needs. The reflective practitioner recognises this reasoning and chooses professional conduct that prohibits emotional dependency and instead facilitates a working relationship that values the service-user's social autonomy. In doing this, however, one must be careful not to sacrifice the distinguishing qualities associated with social care practice, such as altruism, empathy, respect and inclusion. In an analysis of professional identity and relationships, Davies (2003) and MacDonald (2006) compared old and new identity practices. Both argue that establishing a professional identity that sets oneself apart from others (i.e. as the expert) leads to detachment and emotional control. Although both authors' views were considered in the context of professional relationships with other colleagues, similar attitudes and can arise between professional carers and service-users. By rethinking the role and involvement of the service-user, one can value the service-user as an individual who 'belongs' rather than one who simply 'receives' care. This can be extremely challenging for a care worker as she attempts to understand the service-user's point of view while providing support, well-being and empowerment.

Sociological issues highlighted in this practice scenario include: social status, social mobility, social categorisation, social boundaries and social dependence.

PSYCHOLOGICAL PERSPECTIVE
From a psychological perspective, 'transference' applies to this scenario in that Owen reminds Karen of her brother Tom, influencing her relationship with Owen. Originating in Freud's psychoanalytic psychology, transference refers to the unconscious redirection of feelings for one person, often from childhood, to another. It involves the revisiting of past relationships in current situations, the repetition of patterns of relating. Transference is a common experience often anchored in childhood experiences involving feelings associated with repressed experiences rekindled towards another person (Mikulincer & Shaver, 2005). Transference can be positive, inducing emotions such as warmth, admiration or love. Conversely, it can be negative, invoking feelings of hostility, mistrust or dislike. For example, someone who perceived her mother as uncaring and unloving in the early years seeing a social care professional as uncaring and unloving. Someone distrusting another person because they remind them of someone with whom they had a negative experience (in childhood), or being overly friendly and trusting of someone who is reminiscent of a childhood friend. Other examples include someone who immediately dislikes a work manager because they remind them of a teacher they never got on with, or someone being inappropriately dependent upon someone who resembles their mother. Much psychological attention has also been paid to the role of transference in romantic attachments and friendships.

In a therapeutic relationship, transference may be beneficial. The redirection of a child or service-user's feelings from a parent to a care professional may help the service-user to express and resolve feelings. In this context, the professional needs to help 'contain' these feelings and assist the person they are caring for in reflecting on and accepting their feelings, what these mean and the memories they evoke. The professional should never take such feelings personally, or respond in a 'knee-jerk', unthinking fashion. Rather, they need to reflect with the service-user on what has happened, supporting them to consider their feelings anew.

The descriptive point in the scenario that 'sometimes facilitators can feel angry, sad or overwhelmed by what is said' suggests the role of counter-transference. Counter-transference is a *response* to transference, a redirection of a therapist's or professional's unconscious feelings onto a service-user. Manifestations of transference arouse reactions in the other person, related to past life experience. It is this 'emotional entanglement' with another person, which, if expressed or acted upon can cause serious misunderstandings in a relationship. In its widest sense, emotional entanglement refers to 'the emotions, attitudes and patterns of relating which the therapist may begin to experience and enact in the context of a therapeutic relationship' (Flaskas, 2005, p. 129). An example of counter-transference is a professional who avoids a particular service-user because they remind him/her of a difficult sibling. Another example could occur when a professional discourages a service-user from rebuilding their relationship with their father because the professional does not get on with their own father. Alternately, a professional who did not receive enough maternal attention could then perceive a service-user as being too distant, and end up resenting the service-user because of this also reflects counter-transference. Finally, it can also refer to instances in which a professional, such as Karen, literally takes on the problems of the service-user, including their symptoms such as an addiction, depression or paranoia. For further discussion on counter-transference see Winnicott's theory of counter-transference and care practice, as explored by Dennehy (2006).

All of this highlights how important it is for Karen to show self-awareness, a matter discussed earlier in Practice Scenario Six. Professionals need to be acutely aware of the feelings evoked in them by the service-user to make sense of, and use of, their own emotional responses to service-users. In addition, such feelings can also be 'blind-spots' which can impair a professional's empathy, understanding and care, as well as their relationship with the service-user. It is critical that professionals contain these emotions and don't act them out or respond inappropriately (Carpy, 1989).

An understanding of counter-transference is important not only for the professional to regulate his/her emotions but also to help to understand service-users better. It may explain how and why the service-user is trying to elicit a specific reaction in him/her and the basis for this in the service-user's (or professional's) past experience. When a professional's emotions mirror those of the service-user, they can help the professional to understand the feelings that remain unexpressed by the service-user. As Salzberger-Wittenberg (1970, p. 18) noted:

> A client may evoke great concern in us as if the child in him was crying out for maternal care although he may tell us repeatedly that he doesn't want any help. Or, for instance, feeling despair after a client left may be the only clue, that behind the client's outburst of anger there is a hopeless, miserable part of himself.

Feelings can thus be useful in guiding a professional in their care practice (Carpy, 1989). Indicators of transference and counter-transference include: strong feelings of affection or disaffection; a desire to please or avoid; feeling either special or insignificant; over- or under-involvement with a person; feelings of comfort or discomfort with another person and a preoccupation with another and/or power struggles (Jones, 2005).

Caution needs to be exercised, however, in the consideration of transference and counter-transference. Many believe that transference and counter-transference do not exist, in other words, that they are not 'real phenomena'; research can neither prove nor disprove the existence of transference or counter-transference, as they operate at an subconscious level. In common with other psychoanalytic concepts, transference and counter-transference lack scientific evidence and rigour; how 'real' they are is contentious (Bateman, 2004).

Boundaries

Boundaries are nebulous, elusive and difficult to define, but in a general way the term refers to the parameters or limitations on behaviour which enable a safe connection between the professional and the service-user that is always based on the latter's needs (Peterson, 1992). Some boundaries are clearly defined and agreed, such as those laid down in policy and legislation, for example in the *Children First* guidelines. Professional codes also identify boundaries and their violation, and organisational codes of conduct inform employees about boundaries the organisation expect adherence to across various areas of behaviour. Responding to disclosures, the use of discipline and incident reporting are some examples of these. As a professional trains and gains more experience, their boundaries change. Boundaries also change with different jobs, over time and across cultures with changes in norms and in 'what is acceptable or not'.

A 'boundary violation' occurs when a professional places his or her own needs above those of the service-user, which can often appear to be harmless, beginning as an innocent situation that is not recognised as a violation (ibid.). At other times though, these same behaviours may be seen as less serious, in other words, a 'boundary breach'. Karen's increasing friendship with Owen might be considered an example of this. Many see care professionals as having relationship 'boundary styles' along a continuum between the polar extremes of enmeshed and rigid relationships (Davidson, 2005). Professionals with *rigid* boundaries tend to be 'cold', insensitive and distant. They work according to their own agenda and are inflexible and intransigent in what they do. Such rigidity accentuates the power differential between them and the service-user. Professionals with *enmeshed* boundaries are over-involved with service-users, and may have a sibling-like or friendly relationship in which each person needs the other equally. Karen might be seen as leaning more towards this extreme. The question might be asked, 'Who is caring for whom?' When the lines have become blurred such that the professional may be seen as more a friend, mother-figure or girlfriend, this can create false expectations and diminish professional integrity. Outside of legislation, policies, protocols and ethical codes, boundaries can also be identified in a job role by considering the following questions.

1. What is appropriate for me at this stage of my training and in my current occupational role? What am I competent and not competent to do, either on my own or under supervision? Under what circumstances or for which tasks do I need the assistance of another person? Answering these questions enables you to set the limits or boundaries on your competencies.

2. Is there any conflict of interest in what I am doing? Have I something to gain from my relationship with or care of the service-user that places my own personal needs above theirs? It is very important to be able to identify the line between the service-user's benefit and your own benefit as a professional. The former should be prioritised without any personal gain undermining the integrity of your professional role. In the language of ethics, service-users should never be a 'means to an end' for a professional; if they are, then a boundary has been violated (Charleton, 2007).

3. What should be 'private' and what should be 'public' in my relationships with service-users? Where do I draw the line in what I disclose about myself and in what I disclose to others from what a service-user has told me, even in confidence? In this practice scenario, Karen is cautious about revealing too much about herself to her colleagues. Personal discretion and experience will dictate heavily how much a professional discloses

about themselves to colleagues or service-users. With regard to her
colleagues, it is clear that Karen does not yet feel like a part of the team.
Practice Scenario Five discusses team dynamics, which is also pertinent
to this case. In considering disclosure by service-users, the welfare of
the service-user (and others) is critical in deciding when to break
confidentiality. Karen is also deliberating inviting Owen into the sphere
of her personal life to meet her husband Declan, reflecting how her
professional and personal boundaries are becoming blurred and violated,
which deserves serious consideration. How would this affect Karen's
work and Owen's progress? Would this be seen as favouritism by other
service-users? What are some of the questions that would have to be
addressed in coming to a decision on this?

4. What are my own and my organisational professional values? How do
these shape my behaviour and set boundaries on what I do or say in the
work place? Boundaries are demarcated by professional (and personal)
values, and these are often delineated in organisational policies. Values
guide behaviour and 'highlight the worth that certain actions and
practices have which bear them out' (ibid., p. 13). In his book *Ethics for
Social Care in Ireland*, Manus Charleton provides a valuable exploration
of ethics with respect to care practice. Values, such as empowerment,
respect, individualisation of care, dignity and health promotion, are
examples of some of the values in care practice that guide protocols and
boundaries.

5. When do I say 'no' in the work I undertake? One of the most
challenging boundaries is saying no, in knowing and letting others know
what is not possible for you to do as a professional. Everyone needs to
find their own ways to say *no*, ways that do not make the service user feel
alienated or uncared for.

**Psychological issues highlighted in this practice scenario include:
addiction, defence mechanisms, self-esteem and group dynamics.**

PROFESSIONAL PERSPECTIVE
The motivation to work as a professional social care worker is often rooted
in our own life experience. That life experience can be of tremendous value
in adding to the understanding of the worker and their ability to identify
with the service-user. In the practice scenario above, we meet Karen whose
life experience enables her to feel close and build positive relationships with
the people who use the service. It is the closeness of the relationships that
are emerging that raise questions about personal/professional boundaries.
These questions are applicable to all social care worker/service-user

relationships. Our discussion here will examine professionalism in the social care context, the nature of the worker/service-user relationship, 'use of self', and maintaining professional perspective.

Professionalism is often associated with a body of knowledge with academic qualifications as the entrance route. However, social care is one profession where academic knowledge is not the only requirement. Life experience and ability to identify with the service-user group are valuable professional assets. Karen's own upbringing and personal challenges enable her to identify closely with the service-user group. In fact, Karen's personal story may be what attracted her to this kind of work in the first place, and may be recognised as an important aspect of her professional qualification. Deverell and Sharma (2000, p. 25) point out that this aspect of professionalism means that 'professionals may share certain characteristics which decrease, rather than increase, their social distance from clients'. So is this a bad thing?

In our practice scenario, Karen identifies closely with Owen. This closeness is born out of her own life experience and she is considering inviting him and his wife to a social gathering at her house. We see later on that Karen is cautious about revealing 'too much' about her personal background in the group. There are signs here that Karen is struggling to keep a balance between her own needs and those of the group. To gain further insight into this professional dilemma, we visited a community-based drug prevention and support service and sought the views of a worker and service-user there. They both focused on the separation of Karen's personal needs from her professional role. The worker could identify with the challenges that groupwork presents, especially with regards to boundaries. She felt that the questions raised in the group ('Ye know an awful lot about us, but how come we know nothing about ye?') was a common one, best handled sensitively but directly. This could be done by restating the purpose of the group and the role of the worker as facilitator rather than participant. This worker also stressed the need for these roles and boundaries to be set out clearly from the start. Tracing this back further in our practice scenario, the experienced professional pointed to the threefold safety structure of adequate training, organisational support and professional supervision. John Burton, in his excellent *Handbook of Residential Care*, sees supervision and the reasons for it being closely allied to staff support groups. They 'enable workers to work better and to create collective support, understanding and strength to apply to the job in hand' (Burton, 1993, p. 108). Applied to Karen's situation, the absence of staff support (felt by her) and of supervision (evidenced by her professional confusion about 'herself' in the workplace) needs to be addressed.

The service-user we spoke to recognised the personal dimension of Karen's professional role; she also recognised the danger of damaging the group as a whole if these personal issues were not addressed in an appropriate way. This service-user felt strongly that Karen's personal needs could not and should not be addressed in the group. Her blurring of boundaries (by inviting a group member to her house) could cause the group 'to fall apart'. She went on to say that confidentiality is hugely important to the group and that if Karen invites Owen to her house, other participants might feel that their issues were being discussed.

These insights show the importance of clearly established, respected and maintained boundaries. The professional social care role involves creating a therapeutic space in which positive progress can be made. If the worker fills this space with their own concerns, feelings and personal needs, then progress is hindered. Clearly stated, personal/professional boundaries help the worker and service-user to 'keep that working space clear'. Boundaries are there not to put distance between the worker and service-user, but to allow safe closeness in the working relationship.

Karen appears to be highly motivated to help other people. She has chosen a profession that gives her an opportunity to do just that. Indeed, as Bernstein (1999, p. 4) put it, 'most of us need to do work that makes us feel good about ourselves, work that we see as valuable'. And so the questions remain, 'How much of 'ourselves' do we bring to the workplace, and how much is left outside?' A starting point for Karen and all social care professionals in answering this question is offered by Hawkins and Shohet (1998, p. 5) in their discussion on supervision. They state their belief that 'all supervision begins with self supervision and this begins with appraising one's motives and facing parts of ourselves we would normally keep hidden (even from our own awareness) as honestly as possible'. If Karen is to begin to explore her motivation for choosing and staying in this kind of work, she will need the help and support of her agency. Supervision is not an 'added extra' for social care work; it must be seen as an integral part of the job. It is perhaps surprising that many helping organisations and social care workers themselves continue to work without regular or adequate supervision. Without having a space in which to explore the impact of work on the worker, or of the worker on work, there is a higher risk of boundaries blurring in a haze of personal and professional confusion.

Professional issues highlighted in this practice scenario include: establishing and maintaining boundaries and understanding 'use of self' in workplace supervision.

8

Confidentiality

- Over 5,000 children were in the care of the state in 2008.
- The District Court granted 1,201 Care Orders in 2007, representing a rise over past years.
- Most children are taken into care because they have been neglected by parents or guardians. Other reasons include physical, emotional or sexual abuse, behavioural problems and mental health problems. Most children taken into care are placed with foster carers or relatives, but a significant number are taken into residential care homes.
- National standards for children's residential centres and special care units in Ireland were published in 2001.
- Civil society is defined as the public arena in which diverse individuals practice citizenship as they engage and act together in civic actions for the common good. (O'Ferrall, 2002).
- Civil society includes at its core, the values of active citizenship, the values of openness, the values of fairness and equality, the values of solidarity and tolerance (O'Ferrall, 2002).

Practice Scenario 8

Setting: Residential Childcare

Jane is a social care graduate who began working in Forest View children's home two months ago. It is in the same village as where she lives and is near to the shop where she sometimes does some extra work. She recognises some of the children who live in Forest View from the shop. Jane has settled in and works closely with her colleagues on the care team, although she has yet to contribute at staff team meetings. She recognises the importance of working cooperatively with her colleagues and is quietly learning the value of teamwork and cooperation. Although still lacking in experience and professional confidence, Jane gets on very well with the children who live in Forest View and is building a particularly good relationship with Michael, a twelve-year-old boy who arrived a week after Jane started.

Michael was placed in residential care as a result of repeated breakdowns of foster care arrangements. He has had very little contact with his biological parents. He does see his maternal grandmother occasionally and looks forward to visits with her. During most visits, he and his grandmother have little to talk about, but she always takes him shopping for a new jacket, pair of runners or tracksuit, even though he is well looked after. Moving from home to home, Michael has very little that he considers 'his own', as his belongings were often left behind in his various moves across care placements.

While Michael normally hates brushing the yard and doing other chores, he doesn't find it so bad when Jane is there with him as they talk a lot about the soccer team they both follow. Michael has had difficulty trusting adults in the past but sees Jane as someone to whom he can talk. She seems different to other carers or foster parents, and Michael thinks that Jane favours him over the other children in the home, perhaps because the other children have regular contact with their families, and he is often without a visit for weeks at a time.

Recently a music CD went missing in Forest View. Allegations and suspicions were flying everywhere. Jane spotted the missing CD in Michael's room. When she approached him, he denied all knowledge of it or how it got there. Then he said he would tell her if she promised not to tell anyone else. Jane responded that she would have to report it, but then relented when Michael became upset, saying that he would run away if she told anyone about their conversation. Michael explained that the CD reminds him of his younger brother who died two years earlier. He and his younger brother had been in foster care 'for as long as he could remember' and had always 'stuck together'. Since losing his brother, none of the foster placements Michael had worked out. Jane thinks that her colleagues are not fully aware of the degree of Michael's grief. She is unsure what to do and while she knows she should talk with her supervisor about it, she finds it hard to talk with him.

For further consideration...

1. How might the other children and staff in Forest View feel about Jane's relationship with Michael?
2. Why might Michael have difficulty in trusting others?
3. Identify some examples of when it is appropriate or not to keep a service user's secret.
4. How can Jane encourage principles of participation and empowerment with Michael?
5. How does Michael's position in society either empower or disadvantage him at present?

6. What possible consequences might result from withholding information in this case?
7. What possible outcome(s) might result from its disclosure?
8. How might knowledge of family systems theory influence Jane on a professional level?

SOCIOLOGICAL PERSPECTIVE

In social science, the area of confidentiality is an agreed responsibility that frames the formal codes of conduct in research and practice for most sociological associations. In order to safeguard issues arising from inequalities of power or possible conflicts of interest, personal information, records and privileged files of all participants are to be respected and protected (see for example, Sociological Association of Ireland, 2004; Association for Applied and Clinical Sociology, 2006). As a way of exploring the scenario above, it is useful to look at societal values and norms that impact the structure of our social relationships from a broader sociological perspective. Although a framework is established for ethical social research and procedures, there has been, in recent Irish history, a part of the social and political culture that has transgressed issues of confidentiality and principled social practice. Some might describe specific instances (e.g. clerical abuse, blood transfusions or property development) as careless, while others might view them as corrupt, neglectful or exploitative due to the mismanagement of trust and/or funds. Regardless of one's point of view, the controversy has lead to social indignation and calls for organisational change and heightened transparency. Public and private organisations are now scrutinised by individuals, watchdog groups and officials who query decisions and processes in order to ensure uncompromised care, reliability and equity for vulnerable individuals and groups. There is a new emphasis on policy that sets out to guarantee (as much as is possible) social protection and representation for powerless and exposed members of society. Changes in the culture of formal organisations have affected the values, norms and patterns of action that characterise participants' social relationships. Positions of power within organisations are now more likely to be attached to systems and structures of accountability and responsibility and are expected to be aligned with wider social standards and objectives.

Civil society

Parallel to the recent policy and organisational changes in Ireland came a restored interest in what sociologists refer to as 'civil society'. Civil society reflects the activities and culture of self-organised groups addressing community issues. It is based on active citizenship and participation in decision-making processes leading to the empowerment of the citizen (Powell & Guerin, 1999). A further use of civil society in sociological discourse is one that views civil action as counterbalancing the state, thereby preventing it from dominating society (Tovey & Share, 2007). Civil society is largely recognised as social engagement that respects difference and values rational arguments to solve problems. It rejects the prioritisation of individual interests and instead focuses on the collective social good. Examples of civil society include: the family, education, voluntary associations and other non-economic social institutions. Because civil society, by its very definition, requires a degree of mutual trust, what happens when this trust is violated? How is broken trust or broken cooperation transformed once again into collective participation with an agreed action? O'Carroll (1998), Peillon (1998) and Tovey and Share (2007) suggest that with the loss of trust (due to the various scandals mentioned above) members of Irish society have increased their reliance on social solidarity as well as a moving towards increased dependence in both statutory and voluntary sectors.

In the practice scenario, Jane is working within an agency where trust, confidence and professionalism are paramount. She is faced with specific confidentiality issues in relation to her practice. Not only must she consider her duty of care to Michael, but also her professional relationship with colleagues, including her supervisor. In Jane's case, her decision whether or not to disclose information about Michael and the missing CD is, in part, influenced by the rules and expectations (i.e. norms) that guide the behaviour of the care team and service users in Forest View. Additionally, Jane must reflect on what she and others consider as 'good' or 'bad' practice (i.e. values) in relation to withholding or disclosing information that has been shared in confidence. Sociology describes rules, behaviour and expectations as being learned through socialisation. Knowing what is expected, however, does not necessarily guarantee a desired outcome. Jane's decision will merit a subsequent response by colleagues who will accept, criticise or ignore the outcome.

Social control

Whenever an individual or group take a decision affecting other people's lives, power is a factor. Sociologists are interested in meanings of power in both formal and informal relationships and the resulting influence of any power upon social norms. The well-known work of Max Weber (1978; originally 1921) describes power as not only the ability to initiate action but, more importantly, to achieve the desired outcome despite resistance from others. An ethical framework for social care that works against oppression requires attention to relationships of power in society at large (especially between dominant and minority groups), within social care organisations, as well as power relationships between service-users and social care professionals (Clifford & Burke, 2005). Power needs to be considered at different social levels, namely, 'at the level of political, social and economic structures, and at the level of personal power arising from cultural, institutional and psychological factors. Power may be exercised over people tacitly or overtly, but may also be actively produced and wielded by individuals and groups in the context of changing local and national discourses' (ibid., p. 685).

Sociologists are particularly interested in how universal structures of social division and inequality influence how power is allocated and exercised in society. Social justice and oppression are sociological ethical concerns. Social care practitioners need to be able to recognise how unequal power relations are acted out at an interactional level between groups and communities as well as within social care organisations (ibid.).

If Jane's actions are considered inappropriate or unacceptable by the care team, existing power and social control (by members of her team) will most likely influence the development and progress of her working relationships. As social control aims to establish conformity amongst social actors, those who fail to comply are sometimes labelled as deviant. It is important to note, however, that deviance is not necessarily identified by a particular action, but rather by the responses or disapproval of that action by a significant number of people in the social group. In other words, Jane's action, whether to uphold Michael's confidence or to share her concerns with colleagues, may warrant either approval or disapproval in her professional sphere. In the wider sociological setting, some deviant behaviour is branded by informal networks of control (i.e. friends, family, colleagues) while other behaviour is identified through formal controls, such as the criminal justice system. Regardless of which structure identifies behaviour as deviant, it is more likely to occur when particular associations are weak between an individual and society (or in the scenario above, between Jane and her working relationships).

Hirschi (1969) argued that there are four types of bonds connecting people to approved behaviour. They are: attachment, commitment, involvement and belief. Jane must consider whether she is constrained more by her pledge to Michael to protect his 'secret' or by her commitment to her professional colleagues and role as a practitioner. In doing so, Jane must consider three key perspectives: the law, social care principles of practice and ethics. By looking at each of these areas, the issue of confidentiality and disclosure becomes complicated. In addition, her decision will have a consequential impact on Michael.

Jane is trained to recognise the value and application of family systems theory. She understands the impact on Michael of his brother's death and the difficulty of considering one family member in isolation from others. Jane may feel that certain information should be shared with her supervisor and/or colleagues. She also realises that if consulted, Michael would most likely disagree. Jane must gently explore Michael's reasons for refusing and then determine her plan of action. She may sacrifice her alliance to one party in order to preserve the other, or she may establish grounds of trust that will result in the reinforcement of her social care identity and role in Forest View children's home.

Sociological issues highlighted in this practice scenario include: the concept of a 'civil society', social participation, active citizenship and social control.

PSYCHOLOGICAL PERSPECTIVE

One of the striking features of this scenario, from a psychological perspective, is Michael's loss and grief over his brother. In experiencing loss, a person endures deprivation of some kind, the absence of someone or something. While frequently associated with death, as a term, 'loss' has a much broader meaning, and is used in understanding loss of a job, loss of esteem and so forth. Like loss, 'grief' has a much broader meaning than its association with death alone. Grief 'is the process through which one passes in order to recover from a loss' (Fahlberg, 1991, p. 141) and has been outlined earlier in Practice Scenario Three.

Grief is known to include a diverse range of physical and psychological symptoms, including sleep and eating disturbances, poor health, and social withdrawal. Feelings of shock, yearning, helplessness, fatigue and sometimes relief are common in grief (Worden, 1991). Guilt may be a feature of grief if the person feels they brought the loss on themselves or contributed somehow to it. This is often a factor that needs to be addressed with children in care. Currer (2007) emphasised the dual-process model of coping with loss based on work by Stroebe and Schut (1995). This model sees two sequences present in coping with loss: a 'loss orientation' – including grief work – remembering the loss (the person/circumstances) and accepting it, and a 'restoration orientation'. The latter describes when the person deals with changes associated with the loss, copes with the aftermath and readjusts to altered circumstances. Socialisation and culture effects the balance between these orientations (how much one focuses on one or the other).

While Michael has experienced loss in the form of the death of his brother, he, like many other children in care, has also experienced an 'ambiguous loss' – a loss which does not have finality (Boss, 2006) because he has lost his 'normal' family life. This can involve either the physical absence yet psychological presence of someone (e.g. the family of a child in care) or the physical presence but psychological absence of someone (e.g. loss of someone as they have dementia, mental illness). According to Boss (2006), six therapeutic goals inform working with people with ambiguous loss, and these include:

- **Finding meaning**: helping the person to 'make sense' of their loss.
- **Building a sense of control/mastery**: tackling feelings of powerlessness and helplessness.
- **Reconstructing identity**: strengthening a person's sense of self, who they are and where they belong, all of which might have been compromised by the loss.
- **Normalising ambivalence**: the need to live with tension and recognise ambiguity.
- **Revising attachment**: re-understanding and re-working the attachment.
- **Discovering hope**: building optimism within a realistic framework, identifying strategies for growth.

Jane could help to forge a stronger relationship between Michael and his maternal grandmother. This may help Michael to deal with his grief and support his identity and sense of continuity in belonging to a family. It could also reduce the risk of Michael losing all meaningful contact with his immediate and extended family, a common consequence of moving into residential care (Craig et al., 1998). Life story work and having a 'memory box' may also be beneficial for Michael to add to and store all his own things from his past. All of these measures would also help address any concerns that Michael has about his biological family (Ryan & Walker, 1993).

The importance of recognising and endorsing the need to grieve cannot be overemphasised. Feeling that someone is there with you, empathising and 'accompanying you' in your grief and supporting you in readjusting and re-engaging in life (Currer, 2007) would assist Michael to come to terms with his loss. However, this takes time and in the words of Meenan (2005, p. 227):

All residential workers must understand that some young people in residential care may never fully discuss their true feelings or how the emotional impact of their past experiences has affected them. The simplest triggers, such as a song on the radio, a phrase someone uses, the smell of a particular perfume or cologne, may bring memories flooding back. These can be a precursor to a violent outburst or a retreat into their inner space. It is important to let these young people know that there is someone who will be there for them when they feel that they are ready to talk.

Vera Fahlberg's 1991 book, *A Child's Journey Through Placement*, is a very useful text which explores the topic of grief and loss in residential childcare in depth.

Another psychological concern in this case is the need for careful intervention work about inappropriate behaviour, such as stealing. This might be based on the 'life space intervention' (LSI) model. Developed from the psychoanalytic work of August Aichorn (1935), Fritz Redl (1991) developed the concept of 'life space intervention' based on work undertaken with delinquent youths, focusing particularly on their lack of self-control and ineffective use of support. The 'life space' refers to 'direct life experience in connection with the issues that become the interview focus' (Redl, 1966, p. 41) and intervention is based on three premises:

- **Maintain an emotionally healthy environment**: nurture positive interpersonal interaction, show tolerance for deviancy and regressive behaviour, but employ safeguards against escalation. This also involves recognising that children bring their past into their present life (for example, their views on authority figures) and often try to recreate, in their current relationships, the types of relationships they had in their past – transference. They will reuse strategies that they found effective in the past to cope and to get their own way.
- **Enact supportive programmes for psychological development**: programmes can include creative activities, sport and life-story work.
- **The therapeutic management of life events**: using everyday events and incidents to help children gain an understanding of their own behaviour in the context of their past and present life. The focus is kept on what is being said, verbally and nonverbally, without being distracted by other things, including our own feelings and reactions.

From the LSI perspective, inappropriate behaviour, in this case, stealing the CD, often reflects latent developmental anxieties. These include anxieties about:

- **Abandonment**: feeling rejected and that 'no one cares about me'. This is often due to a poor attachment history and expressed in infantile behaviour. Nurturing a sense of security and unconditional affection is important in its treatment.

- **Inadequacy**: self-doubt, low self-esteem, feeling that 'I can't do anything right'. This can be seen in the need to avoid failure, criticism or blame, to cover-up mistakes. Building self-confidence is important in addressing this developmental anxiety.
- **Guilt**: a more complex form of inadequacy in which the person themselves judges themselves to be unworthy: 'I'm not worth it' or 'I'm no good'. It often underlies behaviour such as self-denigration, passive aggression and being scapegoated or exploited. Sometimes, a child may behave inappropriately to prove their own unworthiness with an attitude that says, 'Look! This is me, I'm the worst there is – and I don't care.'
- **Conflict**: difficulty in dealing with conformity and obedience and seeing this as a means of achieving independence. This anxiety is often manifested in aggression and manipulative behaviour and challenging boundaries and work needs to be done on regulating emotions in order to address it.
- **Identity**: concerns about a sense of self, belonging and/or image. Such concerns may permeate a lot of behaviour, particularly in the adolescent years.
- **Roles and values**: Conflict can arise between learned norms and values from past family life and new norms and values in the context of being in care. For example a family that places a high value on independence may have discouraged their child from asking for help; a family in which parents exert little authority may produce a child who has difficulties relating to authority; a family that values being macho and aggressive can hinder a child from seeing that it is possible to be masculine without being aggressive.

While in this practice scenario, the stealing appears to be underpinned by grief for a lost brother, other reasons reflecting the aforementioned anxieties may be present in other cases.

In tackling inappropriate behaviour, it is imperative to consider possible underlying causes. This is outlined in the Department of Health and Children's 'National Standards for Children's Residential Centres'. 'All staff are encouraged to consider the underlying causes of inappropriate behaviour and day-to-day practices are in place to support children in managing their behaviour' (point 6.18). Sometimes young people open up to staff in everyday situations and routines, however 'a quiet space' can also helpful to this. Research by O'Neill (1991, cited in Buckley 2002a) drew attention to the importance of a 'special or quiet room' for children in residential care to share personal information and discuss their situation with their key-worker, notwithstanding the inability of such staff to offer confidentiality on disclosures impacting upon the children's welfare. This room should be used specifically for the promotion of healthy relationship-building using both directive and non-directive approaches. O'Neill (1991) recommended that units should have a policy on confidentiality and promote teamwork in relation to the special room, that the use of time should be led by the children as opposed to being used by staff to deal with behaviour and individual incidents, that key-workers should be empowered to engage more with the families of children and that more options for older children should be explored. Ormonde (1992, cited in Buckley 2002a) found, however, that such a room tended to be used in a haphazard, unsystematic way with little time being spent individually with children in such a space. He stressed the need for such a room to be used therapeutically, for example, using sensory stimuli and play therapy, in ways 'to cultivate an atmosphere of safety and security that would encourage the children to play in an exploratory fashion within a non-threatening environment' (Buckley, 2002a, p. 205).

In addressing inappropriate behaviour, like stealing, professionals also need to be cautious about not being too authoritarian or controlling, ensuring that any sanctions used are humane and appropriate. This is laid down in the 'National Standards for Children's Residential Centres' (DOHC, 6.20–6.24). Care needs to be taken so as not to be too controlling or too humiliating or degrading in any way and any sanctions used should be reasonable and age-appropriate. Michael needs to be encouraged to take more responsibility for, and control over, his own behaviour. As noted by the Irish Social Services Inspectorate (2006, pp. 40–1):

> A preoccupation with control is inimical to good behaviour management. Young people resist and resent being controlled. Most young people, even when they are very troubled, can exercise self-control in certain situations and they should be encouraged and facilitated to do so. … Young people should never 'be made an example of' by care staff anxious to convey a message to other young people in the centre about the unacceptability of some piece of behaviour.

Psychological issues highlighted in this practice scenario include: the practice of secrecy, moral development, and the development of trust in relationships. Resilience is another psychological consideration visible in this case. This was elaborated on earlier in Practice Scenario One.

PROFESSIONAL PERSPECTIVE

Confidentiality features prominently in all social care and social work codes of ethics (see, for example, IASCW, IASW, BASW). Within these codes, it is usually located under a subheading of 'responsibilities to service-users' or similar wording. This indicates that confidentiality is part of the professional responsibility carried by the social care agency and by the individual social care worker (see Figure 3.1). Most authors agree that confidentiality is based upon a basic right of the service-user (Biestek 1957; O'Farrell, 1999; Thompson, 2002). Definitions of confidentiality usually make reference to the trusting relationship between service-user and worker and to the legal and ethical issues that surround its preservation. It is often linked to privacy and located as a professional skill in the context of residential childcare (Hendy & Beresford, 1996, in O'Doherty, 2005). Handling information sensitively and appropriately is further discussed as a particularly challenging skill to master for the inexperienced residential care worker. Ward and colleagues (2003) point out that some young people are adept at manipulating events and situations towards collusive relationships.

Figure 3.1

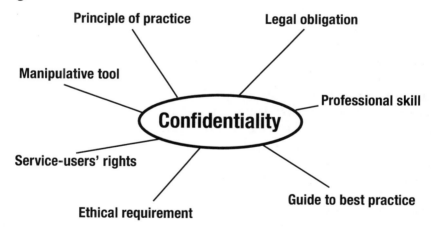

The practice scenario at the beginning of this chapter presents a situation in which Jane, an inexperienced social care worker, becomes somewhat isolated from her colleagues in responding to an incident in a residential care setting. In examining why this professional isolation has happened, the role of how two different types of information are handled becomes the focus of attention. Firstly, information held on file regarding Michael and, secondly, the new and evolving information regarding the missing CD.

Information on file

In residential childcare (as in practically all professional social care settings) information about the service-user is held in confidential files. This can help promote continuity of care and understanding of behaviour, actions/reactions and progress. Who has access to these files and how the information contained in them is used needs careful attention and planning. A residential care manager who commented on this case pointed out that Jane appeared not to have the full picture regarding Michael's background and what other staff did or did not know. She went on to explain that part of her role as a manager combines supporting both residents and staff in meeting the expectations of both. Worthington (2004) talks about the 'integration of the whole' in relation to residential community settings; the actions, reactions, trust and relationships that are constantly evolving need a context. 'The management of boundaries of confidentiality is a crucial element in this: how they are established; what is or isn't regarded as confidential and where, on what basis and how sensitive issues are taken from one context and placed in another are important' (ibid., p.172). Perhaps a task at Forest View is to examine how staff and young people living there are included in the holding of sensitive information on the residents.

Evolving information

'The need to examine our views on confidentiality, or the limits we have placed on it may arise in respect of a particular person or situation' (O'Farrell, 1999, p. 116). Jane is forced to think on her feet when Michael becomes upset as she explains that she will have to report the CD being found in his room. On reading this case, a residential manager and a young person living in residential care offered her sharply contrasting advice:

> *Residential Manager's comment:* 'Jane has reacted impulsively and needs to rethink her decision [not to report her conversation with Michael]. Her response was an emotional one, 'patching-up' an immediate situation. Perhaps she can talk with Michael later, explain why she needs to report the incident and offer to go with him to discuss and find a solution with the manager.'
>
> *Teenage resident:* 'Take the CD ... Give it back to its rightful owner and let yer man Michael run away if he wants to! Thieves should be reported!'

Both pieces of advice, though very different, share one common feature: Jane's professional role in responding to this situation needs to take account of a wider context. The skills of managing information are concerned with knowing what information goes where. Managing information is not an individual task but a team responsibility. This professional skill is at the core of helping relationships, and because of this it is likely to be tested by service-users.

One form of residential childcare is provided in therapeutic communities (see Ward et al., 2003 for definitions). Describing how private and sensitive information is managed in this context may offer guidelines to Jane and Forest View as a whole. Worthington (2004, p. 173) explains that for all children in care, it should be made clear that documentation and reports held on file were shared and discussed with all adult care staff and would be 'thought about, looked after and contained by them'. He also explained that information shared with a particular member of staff would also be shared with other staff. This level of clarity ensured that all staff were included in understanding each child, and that staff could not be split off from the wider staff team by colluding in secret information.

These descriptions of how information is handled may not suit all care settings but they do illustrate the thought and careful planning needed to provide both worker and service-user with a safe context in which to build the working relationship. This planning is rooted in the overall mission and ethos of the helping organisation. Confidentiality, therefore, is not a single skill but encompasses a range of competencies concerned with the handling of different kinds of information. As Biestek (1957) puts it, 'The trust of the worker is developed gradually as the result of a lot of little things.'

Professional issues highlighted in this practice scenario include: the helping relationship, achieving positive change and the role of the social care worker.

9

Non-Judgemental Practice

- There are over 3,000 prisoners in custody in Ireland. Most prisons operate at or near full capacity.
- Over 90 per cent of prisoners are male and the majority are aged 21–40 years.
- Drug offences are one of the main reasons for committal to prison; numbers committed for these offences have risen over recent years. Prisons are one of the largest initiators of methadone treatment nationally.
- Approximately 15 per cent of all women and 6 per cent of all men suffer domestic abuse; of these, only one in three women and one in twenty men report it to the gardaí (Irish Prison Service, 2006; National Crime Council/ESRI, 2005).

Practice Scenario 9:

Setting: Community Day Project for Ex-offenders

Tina is a 30-year-old single mother attending a community day project for ex-offenders. Here she is learning how to get back on her feet after prison life and acquiring return-to-work, computing and budgeting skills. Counselling and welfare assistance are also available. Tina recently completed a two-year sentence for drug and prostitution offences and is now on a methadone programme, as she has history of drug abuse. Tina's partner, Damien, is in prison for robbery and due out in the coming year. Tina visits him regularly in prison and brings him drugs when she can. Damien was violent towards Tina when they lived together. Tina's two children, Justin and Christina, aged six and five, are being looked after by Tina's mother, Debbie, in her own home. Tina feels compelled to visit the day project to keep her probation officer or social worker happy. She gets on well with the staff there including Mary, one of the project leaders, and Aoife, the support worker who is her key-worker. Aoife is keen to help Tina to look after her children again, though this isn't a priority for

Tina, who just wants to have a flat for herself and Damien when he gets out. Tina told Aoife, 'Being with Damien is what matters to me. I know he has his problems but so do I, and he loves me anyhow. The kids are grand with their granny. They don't need me like Damien does.' Aoife can't understand why Tina would want to go back to someone who has battered her and is a drug abuser. Aoife feels that Tina needs help to realise that she can be a very good mother, and that her children need her more than Damien does. She tries to get Tina to visit her children more, but, usually, Tina agrees and then pulls out an excuse at the last minute and doesn't go. When returning home in a cab after a late night out over the weekend, Aoife spotted Tina at a street corner, dressed up and looking like she was engaging in prostitution again. Aoife thinks that she should tell Mary, her project manager about this when she comes in on the next shift, but is unsure. She is equally unsure as to whether to raise it with Tina as well.

For further consideration...

1. What assumptions do you think Aoife has about Tina and Damien?
2. What advice do you think Mary would give to Aoife?
3. What might Tina's children, Justin and Christina, be feeling about their relationship with Tina, Damien and Debbie?
4. What concerns might professionals hold about Justin and Christina's welfare and development?

SOCIOLOGICAL PERSPECTIVE

Social roles are a key concept in sociology, one that links an individual's behaviour with agreed expectations in a particular social situation. One's position in society (be it as a parent, doctor, student, etc.) often influences the anticipated behaviour. When exploring social roles and their impact on individuals, groups or society in general, one considers how an identifiable role is given status or is allocated rights, privileges or responsibilities. Sociologists take particular interest in cases in which multiple roles are interwoven, thereby combining the interaction that evolves from standards, duties and rights associated with the various roles. Sometimes roles become socially incompatible, producing conflict or inconsistency. For example, in the scenario above, one of Tina's roles is motherhood, in addition to her roles of partner, daughter, service-user and ex-prisoner. Her experiences and feelings, when acting in these roles, are most likely mixed and perhaps contradictory. Recent Irish research shows that most prison mothers have difficulty coming to terms with their dual (or multiple) roles and as a result develop coping mechanisms that serve to alleviate uncertainty and distress caused by custodial sentences (McCann James, 2001; 2004).

Familial ties and prison peer influence

A repetitive theme in sociological literature regarding women prisoners suggests that they suffer increased anguish because of worries about family, especially their children. Women prisoners are continually challenged because of geographical and emotional barriers that disadvantage consistent contact and relational ties with family (Carlen, 1983, 1998; Faith, 1993; Genders & Player, 1987, 1998; Girshick, 1999; Kruttschnitt, 2000; Liebling, 1994; Matthews , 1999; McCann James, 2004; Owen, 1999; Richards et al., 1995; Shaw, 1999). Repeated or extended periods of custody diminish the amount and quality of contact mothers have with their children. Mothers have limited time with children while in custody (i.e. visitation) and most are reliant on the goodwill of family, friends or social workers to organise prison visits resulting in unpredictable arrangements. The Dóchas Centre, Ireland's purpose-built female prison, provides facilities for some women to keep babies with them and for maintaining close contact with their young children. If a woman is pregnant when she arrives in prison, it is possible for her keep her baby with her for up to nine months. In this way, the Dóchas Centre helps to facilitate the bonding between mother and child, in spite of barriers that accompany custodial life. Despite this policy, many mothers are inevitably separated from their children, and meaningful family relationships are difficult to sustain over lengthy periods of time.

Research has found that continued separation from their children is not only painful for mothers but increases their feelings of regret, shame and fear of rejection (Keavey & Zauszniewski, 1999; Pennix, 1999; Young & Jefferson Smith, 2000). Women in prison or with custodial histories are anxious about being portrayed as 'bad', 'incompetent' or inferior' in the eyes of their children. They worry that the mother–child relationship will deteriorate if, or when, children realise that their mother is a convicted criminal. The role of motherhood is therefore threatened by imprisonment, and many mothers lose confidence in their ability to mother. As a result, and as a way of coping with their predicament, many mothers distance themselves from their children and other family members, developing alternative relationships with prison peers. These changes to social relationships lead to increased emotional distance between mothers and their children and intensified dependence upon prison allies. This is especially evident in women who experience repeated or extended periods in custody. As a consequence, prison relationships progressively reinforce prisoners' values as the women's contact and relationships with friends and family outside of prison become less central to their identity while in prison (McCann James, 2004). 'Prisoners' values' here refers to the social beliefs held by members of a prison group or community. These values shape the behaviour of individuals within the group and influence the approval or disapproval of specific conduct. Social values can vary from one group to another and may also change depending upon circumstances or social conditions.

Violence against women

This practice scenario has resonances with Practice Scenario Four as both involve domestic violence/abuse. Tina appears to lack motivation to engage regularly in the care of her two young children. She is much more focused on her relationship and future with her partner, Damien, than her attachment to her children. Aoife, Tina's care worker, is concerned about the mother–child bond; however, the matter is complex and merits an understanding of what sociologists identify as role conflict or role strain. Robert Merton's (1957) analysis of social structures and cultural values demonstrated that even with definite pressures to conform, individuals faced contradictions that make deviance their necessary outcome. Applying Merton's argument, Tina abandons her role as mother because she views conforming to society's expectation of motherhood as unattainable. She has discarded the approved profile of motherhood and retreated to an alternative lifestyle that values drug use and condones or necessitates prostitution. By substituting her allegiance to Damien over that to her children, Tina manifests what Durkheim (1933, originally published in 1893) referred to as 'anomie', or disorder and meaninglessness in her life, as compared to a well-ordered confirmation of societal expectations.

Although most female prisoners in Ireland are mothers, most do not consider motherhood to be a primary feature in determining their choice of prison alliances. Instead, women arrange social connections around common behaviour, attitudes and social expectations. When women leave prison and return to their homes and communities, relationships have often been compromised and sometimes even abandoned. Tina appears reluctant to engage actively with her own mother or as a mother herself with her two children. Research shows that when women renegotiate their social position and function in an attempt to manage their custodial situation, they rely on the prison culture and its resources for relief from the physical, social and emotional deprivation that accompanies imprisonment (McCann James, 2004). Tina is now out of prison but still struggling with her social identity and social expectations as a mother, daughter, partner and recovering substance abuser. Her choices may be heavily influenced by her previous drug addiction and/or her current dependence on methadone. Another factor to consider is that Tina may feel more in control of her life when she is with Damien than when she is with her children. She may believe that life with Damien is predictable and that she is able to manage better with him than with her mother or children. Women who live in violent relationships are often held responsible for the violence committed against them. Rather than assigning the blame to the perpetrator and identifying the violence as a crime, many (including the women themselves) consider the violence to be deserved or as something that could have been avoided had they behaved differently.

Confusion about responsibility for violence occurs in an ideological context that stresses women's complete dependence upon their partners and is legitimised when women are not afforded equal power in their relationships with men. Sociologists and women's support groups have stressed that violence against women is more effectively understood within the context of women's and girls' subordinate status in society at large. In fact, gender inequality is now deemed to be one of the principle causes of violence against women because women are exposed, by virtue of their gender, to physical, sexual and/or psychological abuse (Women's Health Council, 2007). Recent Irish statistics show that 67 per cent of violence against women is committed by 'intimate males'. Intimate males are defined as a current or former spouse, co-habitee or partner (Women's Aid, 2006). Despite our contemporary insight into violence against women and the work of dedicated agencies, a social stigma and silence stills surrounds this abuse. Societal culture and structures can be identified as unintentionally colluding with perpetrators, effectively trapping women in abusive relationships. Women's safe options are destroyed by under-resourced and insufficient secure women's shelters, lack of education or employment options and a fear of losing custody of their children.

Social control and exploitation

In addition to the effects of violence against women, sociology also acknowledges labelling as a tool used to socially control women in society. Labelling is a theory that identifies deviance as being created by society, rather than by individuals. Theorists such as Becker (1963), Cohen (2002) and Plummer (1979) argued that society agrees on rules of acceptable behaviour. Defiance of approved social rules results in stigmatising individuals who do not conform, often resulting in the offending individual being isolated and excluded from society (in this example, by imprisonment). Sociologists also consider labelling to be responsible for the 'deviant' who defines herself as a social outsider and subsequently associates with others who are similarly labelled, leading to accelerated deviance and further social sanctions. Many women like Tina are labelled as 'drug addicts' and/or 'ex-prisoners' and are left with few, if any, socially approved role options. Women such as Tina can easily find themselves vulnerable, being reduced to sexual objectification by others, be it with or without their consent. Prostitution becomes a further violation of their discredited dignity, self-esteem and confidence. Although international laws and conventions attempt to combat the exploitation of vulnerable women (see for example, Convention on the Elimination of All Forms of Discrimination Against Women, 1979; OHCHR, 1949, 1993), most regional and national governments have failed to protect the explicit abuse and violence suffered by women involved in prostitution. Agencies and groups committed to addressing such exploitation identify women involved in prostitution as members of the most oppressed and vulnerable groups in society. Such women become ensnared in the sex trade because of the lack of viable, reasonable alternatives and those with the fewest alternatives have been identified as the least able to exit prostitution once involved (Ruhama, 2007).

Facilitating change for women such as Tina requires a targeted and integrated approach that identifies social structures and circumstances that subject women to violence. It is vital that support programmes related to education, job training and personal development be properly resourced to enable women to escape violence and leave prostitution. Additionally, public education is necessary to expose the harm caused to women who experience violence – including the exploitation experienced through prostitution. Legal, social and economic frameworks must be in place to address and eradicate flawed ideologies, politics and social practices.

Sociological issues highlighted in this practice scenario include: the impact of repeated custody, social identity and its renegotiation, prison culture, subgroups and regimes, labelling theory and the sociology of gender-based violence.

PSYCHOLOGICAL PERSPECTIVE

Codependency is a term that refers to a 'dependence upon the dependency of another'. The codependent person or 'enabler' consciously and unconsciously supports the perpetuation of the other person's addictive problem (Whitfield, 1987; Beattie, 1989). Characteristics of codependency include: seeking the approval of others, especially, the other person with the addiction, putting the needs of the other before personal needs (or those of others), low self-esteem and a defensive denial of the problems inherent in the relationship. Some theorists see codependency as a legacy of an insecure attachment in childhood resulting in the codependent feeling unloved, unwanted and inadequate. They need to be needed and obsess on the person with the addiction, often to the neglect of themselves and others, including their children. The roots of codependency lie within troubled, enmeshed families where boundaries are diffused and where, so to speak, 'when one person itches everyone scratches'. Often, children raised in an enmeshed, sometimes excessively rigid family, who are extremely compliant and extremely willing to please are seen as very 'good' children. However, being overly compliant early on in life may mean that they learn to neglect their own needs for the love of others. They may learn *not* to assert themselves, in order to feel wanted and loved (Beattie, 1989). Others contend that codependency is not a negative trait per se, rather, it is a personality trait enacted to an extreme. Some psychologists see codependency as a feature of the traditional female gender role which emphasises self-sacrifice and caring for others (Hands & Dear, 1994). Interestingly, codependency in non-clinical populations has sometimes been associated with positive characteristics of family functioning (Layne et al., 1998). In this scenario, Tina appears to be codependent in her relationship with Damien. She is assisting his drug habit by bringing drugs to him in prison and thereby putting her own status at risk. She perceives that Damien appears to need her more than her own children do and because of this prioritises him over her children.

Domestic abuse or violence is also an issue in this scenario as it is in Practice Scenario Four. Domestic abuse has been defined as 'a pattern of physical, emotional or sexual behaviour between partners in an intimate relationship that causes or risks causing significant negative consequences for the person affected' (National Crime Council/ESRI, 2005, p. 23). Approximately one in seven women and one in sixteen men have experienced severely abusive behaviour by a partner at some time in the lives. Parenthood, parental abuse in the family of origin, isolation of persons from their close family and community supports, alcoholism and a relationship in which one person controls decision-making over money are all factors strongly associated with domestic abuse (ibid.). Rather than focusing on individual incidents of violence, psychology tends to look at such violence as a *process* designed to maintain power and control, which is ongoing in the relationship over time.

Figure 3.2 Power and Social Control Wheel

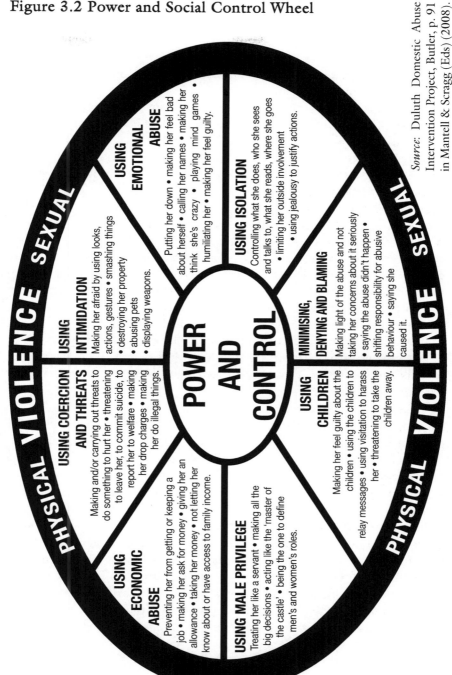

Source: Duluth Domestic Abuse Intervention Project, Butler, p. 91 in Mantell & Scragg (Eds) (2008).

The 'power and social control wheel' (Butler, 2008, p. 91, see Figure 3.2) illustrates some of the strategies and behaviours characteristic of such violence. Research has highlighted that women who experience domestic abuse emphasise the need for safety to be prioritised and for this to be treated as a distinct issue, treated separately from whether or not they stay in the relationship (Abraham, 2007).

The exchange/social control theory of domestic violence (Gelles, 1983) focuses on the 'rewards' and 'costs' of being violent in the family unit. This perspective emphasises the roles of 'internal' (i.e. moral conscience, socialisation, self-regulation, etc.) and 'external' controls (laws, loss of respect, etc.), also called 'inner and outer containment', on determining whether domestic violence is exhibited or not. According to this perspective, people are violent because they *can* be. Violence is seen as more likely when the costs of being violent – being hit back, arrest, imprisonment, dissolution of family unit, being socially ostracised, loss of the partner – are *lesser* than the rewards, which include power, control and self-esteem. The lack of effective social controls, such as legislation and community supports, reduces the costs of family violence. In addition, the cost of losing a partner may be seen as greater than the cost of harming a child.

As highlighted in the South Eastern Health Board Kilkenny incest investigation report (1993), assistant Chief Davies of the English Police Staff College urged awareness of the following factors in understanding why female victims of domestic abuse remain or return to their violent partner.

> She may be in physical fear of her partner … she may fear for her future, for the future of the relationship, for the future of the roof over her head and her income … she may be afraid for her children. It is not infrequent that batterers will batter both wife and child. She may have suffered violence to herself, but not complained to the police because she fears for her child's safety … she may be afraid that her complaint will cause her children to lose their father … she may have nowhere else to go … she may have no money and no support … she may be afraid that she herself will lose her children … she will almost certainly be feeling guilty and wondering whether she is a bad wife or a bad mother … she may feel whatever happened must have been her fault, that she may have provoked the problem … she may despite it all still have affection for her partner and have some wish to save the relationship.
>
> (Davies, 1993 in SEHB, 1993)

In this practice scenario, another focus of psychological attention is parenting and parenting style (the parents' approach to child-rearing). Tina has concerns about her parenting capacity at this point in time. She prioritises her relationship with Damien above her mothering role, feeling that Damien needs her more than her children, whom she feels are doing fine being looked after by her mother, their grandmother. In considering this practice scenario, it is useful to consider Tina's parenting from the perspective of psychological research by Baumrind (1980) on parenting styles. The four main parenting styles are:

- **Authoritative**: high in both warmth and parental control; children raised with this parenting style tend to be energetic, friendly, socially skilled and cooperative.
- **Permissive**: high level in warmth but low in parental control. Children raised with this style tend to be impulsive, aggressive and self-centred.
- **Authoritarian**: low level of warmth, a certain 'aloofness' and a high level of parental control. Children raised with this style tend to be moody, conflicted and irritable.
- **Uninvolved**: low levels of both warmth and control; an aloof and non-controlling parenting style. Children tend to be socially and academically weak, hostile, rebellious and anti-social (Baumrind, 1980; 1991). Tina's parenting style might be categorised as uninvolved.

However, parenting styles are quite broad, general and imprecise. The extent to which any parenting can or should be categorised as any one 'type' is contentious. Parenting styles may change over time and be different between parents and other family carers; they are influenced by the parent's emotional and material resources, social supports, the characteristics of the child and the socio-cultural context (Belsky, 1984). Many psychologists would argue that rather than categorising parenting according to parenting styles, it is more useful to examine parenting according to the features important to a child's development. Such indicators form the basis of parenting assessment interviews and observation schedules. According to Jowitt and O'Loughlin (2005), key indicators of parenting ability identified in parenting assessments by psychologists include:

- **Basic care**: physical needs met, including shelter, clothing, hygiene, medical and dental care.
- **Ensuring safety**: protection from harm and danger.
- **Emotional warmth**: emotional needs met, positive sense of identity, emotional sensitivity and responsiveness, encouragement, praise, comfort, affection, physical contact.

- **Stimulation**: promotion of learning and cognitive development, communication, play, facilitation to achieve, school attendance.
- **Guidance and boundaries**: enabling the child to regulate his/her own emotions and behaviour, demonstrating and modelling behaviour, control of emotions and relating to others. Helping the child to internalise moral norms, develop a conscience and social behaviour appropriate to society. Helping a child to develop problem-solving skills, anger management and learning to judge what to do in various situations. Self-discipline.
- **Stability**: continuity and consistency of relationship; capacity to ensure secure attachments are not disrupted.

These areas also form the basis for parenting programmes to help develop parenting skills and instil confidence in parents like Tina in their own parenting abilities. However, in her role as a care professional, Aoife needs to be careful not to pressurise Tina into undertaking a parenting programme as that is not what she wants at this point in time. Aoife has to be careful not to expect Tina to have the same values that she, Aoife, has regarding parenting or romantic relationships. Aoife must not confuse her personal values with her values as a care professional; just because she would not personally make a choice does not mean that she should not support Tina in making that choice. Rather, Aoife should make Tina aware of all the options and supports open to her, with Tina being cognisant of the possible implications of any decisions she makes.

It is also interesting to consider this case from a 'family systems' perspective, whereby the family is conceptualised as a system, a dynamic unit, an organisation of interdependent, coordinated elements (family members) which influence each other directly and indirectly (Minuchin, 2002). It is embedded within wider systems, such as the extended family, the local community, professional services, social welfare, the media and the culture we live in, all of which influence family functioning (Dunst et al., 1988).

Subsystems within the family system include the marital dyad, the parent–child subsystem and the sibling subsystem. Within each of these subsystems, relationships may vary for individual family members, in that a child or parent may experience very different types of relationships with each of the other family members. For example, a mother may experience her relationship with one child to be engaging and loving, while with another child it may be irritable and tense, and with another child it may be virtually absent, lacking in interaction or closeness. The system is more than the sum of its parts, and thus any consideration of the family necessitates not only reflection on each family member as an individual person but also on:

- relationships within the family, including the degree of closeness and the power structure;
- the impact of each relationship on other relationships in the family;
- family rules, both explicit and implicit, and roles;
- socio-cultural features (e.g. child-rearing practices, policy and values); and
- intergenerational factors (i.e. each parent's experience of the family of origin; attachment history).

(de Róiste, 2006)

In this practice scenario it seems that the family unit has two distinct subsystems: the marital subsystem, consisting of Tina and Damien, and the grandparental subsystem, consisting of Tina's mother and Tina's children. Both of these subsystems appear to be disengaged from each other with little contact between the two parties. This is a concern psychologically, as attachment theory emphasises the importance of a child's early attachment relationships for their mental and emotional development. How family members love and care for each other is a key factor in defining a sense of family for children, over and above structural features, such as sharing the same residence (Nixon et al., 2006). The lack of contact and parenting between Tina and Damien and their children does not auger well for the children's attachment to their parents and their relationships with them in the future. However, the children may be attached to their grandmother, as she may be their primary attachment figure and parenting them adequately. If Tina were to become their primary carer again, the experience might not prove to be positive for either Tina or the children. Perhaps if Damien were there to support Tina, she would be better able to care for the children – or perhaps not.

A school of thought in psychology called 'symbolic interactionism' also draws attention to the significance of the meanings people ascribe to the other people in their lives. In this practice scenario, one wonders what the children actually mean to Tina; do they mean added stress, for example? Does she see them as a threat to her relationship with Damien? Does she see them as reflecting something negative about herself? Do they remind her of something she wants to forget from her own childhood? All of these are possible issues in Tina's relationship with her children.

Psychological issues highlighted in this practice scenario include: bonding and attachment, motherhood and fatherhood and attribution theory.

PROFESSIONAL PERSPECTIVE

Felix P. Biestek first published *The Casework Relationship* in 1957. In this book, he sought to 'explain, define and analyse the casework relationship as a whole and in its parts' (p. viii). Our discussion here focuses attention on non-judgemental practice and the skills associated with it in the social care context. A useful starting point in examining the practice scenario is to reproduce Biestek's definition of a non-judgemental attitude.

> The non-judgemental attitude is a quality of the casework relationship; it is based on a conviction that the casework function excludes assigning guilt or innocence, or degree of client responsibility for causation of the problems or needs, but does include making evaluative judgements about the attitudes, standards or actions of the client; the attitude which involves both thought and feeling elements, is transmitted to the client.
>
> (ibid., p. 90)

In the practice scenario, we see a positive working relationship being built between Tina and her key-worker, Aoife, in spite of the fact that Tina only attends to meet the conditions of her probation order. However, progress appears to be slow or non-existent, and Aoife is unsure of her role. There seems to be some confusion between Aoife's personal and professional feelings about the choices that Tina continues to make. Biestek differentiates between judgements that ascribe blame to the service-user and evaluative judgements that can be useful in helping the service-user to understand the impact of their actions on themselves and others.

> Project worker in support service for ex-offenders' comment: 'People in the community at large often don't understand the client's needs or potential. They [ex-offenders] are all tarred with the same brush. Many people just don't want to know.'

A non-judgemental attitude on the part of the worker can help to create a place of safety and security in which the service-user can explore new goals and possibilities. Egan (1994) identifies three stages of the helping model:

Stage 1: The current state of affairs – clarification of the key issues calling for change.

Stage 2: The preferred scenario – helping clients determine what they need and want.

Stage 3:   Strategies for action – helping clients discover how to get
what they need and want.

(ibid., p. 10)

Aoife has established a working relationship with Tina but has yet to clarify
her own professional role. The professional task here is for Aoife to develop
an understanding of how and where her own values and feelings fit into her
work with service-users. When invited to comment on the case, an ex-
offender we spoke to was quite prescriptive, focusing on what needed to
happen and, in particular, what Aoife should do:

> Ex-offender's comment: 'Aoife should contact social services ... help with a
> drug rehab programme ... contact probation ... [and] confront Tina.'

It appears that Aoife is struggling with what action to take and, for the
moment at least, is paralysed by indecision as she works through her own
feelings about Tina's decisions. A non-judgemental attitude may help to
remove this difficulty, but being non-judgemental in practice demands a
clear understanding of the professional role. Thompson (2002) and others
have made the useful distinction between 'skills' and 'qualities' or
'characteristics'. There are qualities and indeed attitudes that are helpful to
professional social care work (a non-judgemental attitude is one), however,
it is important to identify and recognise skills and skill-sets that can be
learned, developed and practised. The benefits to be gained from
developing our skills in working with people include:

- greater understanding of our work roles and tasks;
- increased likelihood of achieving success;
- decreased potential for making mistakes;
- higher level of confidence;
- greater opportunities for job satisfaction; and
- opportunities for achieving an advanced level of practice.

A general non-judgemental attitude can become an integral part of the
professional social care role when it is supported by and practiced through
particular skills. These skills include:

- **Reflection**: reflection-in-action and reflection-on-action (Schön, 1985).
  To be able to act and then react to what is happening and, later, to look
  back systematically at what has happened.
- **Articulation**: to practise the art of capturing, recording and expressing
  the essence of the work through journaling and supervision.

- **Deeper listening**: listening at different levels to both verbal and non-verbal messages and to communicate that the person is being heard.
- **Expanding the knowledge-base**: To understand the wider contexts and social structures that exist in the working relationship, in addition to the awareness of cultural, economic, class or social assumptions which the worker and service-user may bring with them.

When combined, these skills foster a non-judgemental attitude in the professional context. In the practice scenario, Tina's choices are not ones that Aoife would make, nor even understand. Aoife's role is to help Tina to understand the impact of her choices and to empower her towards making a positive change. This is a step-by-step process, and for Aoife to remain involved, she must begin to understand her own role and her impact on her working relationships.

Professional issues highlighted in this practice scenario include: the helping relationship, achieving positive change and the role of the social care worker.

Appendix
Team Roles
SEE PRACTICE SCENARIO FIVE

The **coordinator** is a person-oriented leadership role. Typically, the coordinator is a good listener, tolerant, trustworthy, accepting, dominant and has a commitment to team goals. This role involves guiding the team towards objectives, showing insight into the strengths and weaknesses of the entire team and how to get the most and best out of everyone. Sometimes, though, this can be perceived as being too manipulative.

The **shaper** is a task-focused, competitive, dynamic leader committed to reaching goals and will coerce or 'shape' others to achieve such goals. The shaper often provokes, challenges and argues with other team members. Having a few shapers in a group often leads to conflict. Shapers and co-ordinators can clash over leadership but can also complement each other.

The role of the **plant** is one of a specialist idea-maker, typically an introvert who displays original, innovative, creative ideas and approaches to problems and issues. Plants have little time for minor details or trivia, as they focus more on major issues and the bigger picture. At times, they may need to be 'brought back to earth' as they can be 'out of touch' with reality.

The **resource investigator** is the team's contact person for dealing with external work. Typically this role requires good communication, sociability and negotiation skills. They explore 'networks', develop contacts and probe others for information or resources from outside the group as needed. However, they are liable to lose interest after the initial enthusiasm has passed.

The **implementer** role (also called 'company worker') is focused, diligent and systematic in work. The implementer is associated with good organisational skills and tends to do the jobs that others don't want. However, they can be conservative, inflexible and slow to respond to new possibilities

The role of **monitor-evaluator** refers to the team member who can be impartial and objective, but typically has a low drive to attain the goal. Monitor-evaluators take their time over decisions and can play a key role in decision-making because of their ability to evaluate in a judicious way. However, this role can be underappreciated, partly because members who fill this role can be excessively critical or cynical, with little to inspire or motivate others. This role complements the role of the plant as they debate over issues.

The **team worker** is typically the diplomat, the individual who keeps the team spirit up and diffuses potential conflict. They tend to have good social skills, a sense of humour and sensitivity to the feelings of others. However, they can also be indecisive and reluctant to do things that might hurt others. Whereas the resource investigator negotiates outside of the team to obtain what the team needs, the team worker facilitates or negotiates within the team.

The **completer** or **finisher** focuses on details and deadlines and is typically meticulous, thorough and consistent in their work. They 'dot the is and cross the ts.' However, they can be perfectionists, overly anxious and often have difficulty letting go and delegating work.

Finally, an additional role identified by Belbin after developing his initial theory is the role of the **specialist**. This individual holds specialist knowledge and skills which are not typically held by others in the team. However, they can be very single-minded, focusing too long on technicalities and often only make a narrow or minor contribution to the team (Belbin, 1993).

References

Abrahams, H. (2007). *Supporting Women after Domestic Violence.* London: Jessica Kingsley.

Age Action Ireland (2007). Age Facts. www.ageaction.ie, accessed on June 2008.

Ahlginer, N.R. & Esser, J.K. (2001). 'Testing the groupthink model: effects of promotional leadership and conformity predisposition'. *Social Behaviour and Personality,* 29: 31–42.

Aichorn, A. (1935). *Wayward Youth.* New York: The Viking Press. (Original work published 1925.)

Archer, J. (1999). *The Nature of Grief: The Evolution and Psychology of Reactions to Loss.* New York: Routledge.

ARK Survey of Ageism and Attitudes to Older People in the Republic of Ireland. Unpublished. Dublin: NCAOP. In: Y. McGivern (Ed.) (2003). Healthy Ageing Conference: Conference Proceedings, Report No. 80. Dublin: NCAOP.

Association for Applied and Clinical Sociology (AACS) (2006). Code of Ethics. www.aacsnet.org/wp/?page_id=47 accessed on 02-11-08.

Ayotte, W. (2000). *Separated Children Coming to Western Europe.* London: Refugee Council & Save the Children Fund, UK.

Baker, J., Lynch, K., Cantillon, S. & Walsh, J. (2004). *Equality: From Theory to Action.* Houndmills: Palgrave.

Balloch, S. & Taylor, M. (2001). *Partnership Working: Policy and Practice.* Bristol: Polity Press.

Banks, S. (2006). *Ethics and Values in Social Work* (3rd Ed.). Basingstoke: Palgrave Macmillan.

Barnardos (2000). 'Meeting the Needs of Refugee and Asylum Seeking Children in Ireland.' Policy document. Dublin: Barnardos National Office.

Barnes, C. (1996). 'Theories of Disability and the origins of the oppression of disabled people in western society'. In: L. Barton (Ed.). *Disability and Society: Emerging Issues and Insights,* pp.43–61. London: Longman.

Barnes, C. (1998). Review of Susan Wendell, *The Rejected Body*. *Disability and Society*, 13, 1: 145–6.

Bateman, A. (2004). 'Psychoanalysis and psychiatry: is there a future?' *Atca Psychiatrica Scandinavia*, 109: 161–3.

Bauman, Z. (1999). *Culture as Praxis*. London: Sage Publications Ltd.

Baumrind, D. (1980). 'New directions in socialization research'. *American Psychologist*, 35: 639–52.

Baumrind, D. (1991). 'Parenting styles and adolescent development'. In: J. Brooks-Gunn, R. Lerner & A. C. Petersen (Eds) *The Encyclopedia of Adolescence*, pp. 746–58. New York: Garland.

Beattie, M. (1989). *Beyond Codependency, and Getting Better All the Time*. San Francisco: Harper/Hazelden.

Bebbington, A. & Miles, J. (1989). 'The background of children who enter local authority care'. *British Journal of Social Work*, 19: 349–68.

Becker, H.S. (1963). *Outsiders: Studies in the Sociology of Deviance*. New York: The Free Press.

Beddoes-Jones, F. (2002). 'Belbin's Team Roles and Cognitive Team Roles: A study of two "perspectives"?', www.ukhrd.co.uk.

Belbin, R.M. (1981). *Management Teams – Why They Succeed or Fail*. London: Butterworth Heinemann.

Belbin, R.M. (1993). Team Roles at Work. Oxford: Butterworth-Heinemann.

Belsky, J. (1984). 'The determinants of parenting: A process model'. *Child Development*, 55: 83–96.

Bernstein, G.S. (1999). *Human Services? ... "That must be so rewarding"*. Baltimore: Health Professionals Press.

Biestek, F. (1957). *The Casework Relationship*. London: Unwin University Press.

Bimead, C. & Cowley, S. (2005). 'A concept analysis of partnership with clients'. *Community Practitioner*, 78, 6: 203–8.

Blaikie, A. (1996). 'From "Immorality" to "Underclass": the Current and Historical Context of Illegitimacy'. In J. Weeks & J. Holland (Eds). *Sexual Cultures: Communities, Values and Intimacy*. New York: St Martin's Press.

Bolton, G. (2005, 2nd Ed.). *Reflective Practice: Writing and Professional Development* London: Sage.

Boss, P. (2006). *Loss, Trauma and Resilience: Therapeutic Work with Ambiguous Loss*. New York: W.W. Norton & Co.

Bowling, A. (2005). 'Ageing Well: Quality of Life in Old Age'. *Growing*

Older. Maidenhead: Open University Press.

Bradley et al. (2002). 'Reported Frequency of Domestic Violence: Cross Sectional Survey of Women Attending General Practice'. *British Medical Journal*, 324: 271–4.

Brandon, M. & Lewis, A. (1996). 'Significant harm and children's experiences of domestic violence'. *Child and Family Social Work*, 1: 33–42.

Brenner, H. & Shelley, E. (1998). 'Adding Years to Life and Life to Years: A Health Promotion Strategy for Older People'. Dublin: NCAOP/DOHC.

Bronfenbrenner, U. (1974). *The Ecology of Human Development: Experiments by Nature and Design*. Cambridge, MA: Harvard University Press.

Brown, B. (2000). *Group Processes*. London: Blackwell.

Buckley, H. (2000a). 'Inter-agency co-operation in Irish child protection work'. *Journal of Child Centred Practice*, 6: 9–17.

Buckley, H. (2000b) 'Working together to protect children: Evaluation of an inter-agency training programme'. *Administration*, 48: 24–42.

Buckley, H. (2002). *Child Protection and Welfare: Innovations and Interventions*. Dublin: IPA.

Buckley, H. (1998). 'Filtering Out Fathers: The Gendered Nature of Social Work in Child Protection'. *Irish Social Worker*, 16, 3: 7–11.

Buckley, H., Skehill, C., & O'Sullivan, E. (1997). *Child Protection Practices in Ireland*. Dublin: Oak Tree Press.

Bunreacht na hÉireann (1937). Dublin: Government Publications.

Butler, G. (2008). 'Domestic violence: Understanding the connections'. In A. Mantell & T. Scragg (Eds). *Safeguarding Adults in Social Work*. Exeter: Learning Matters.

Butler, R. (1975). *Why Survive? Being Old in America*. New York: Harper and Row.

Burton, J. (1993). *The Handbook of Residential Care*. London: Routledge.

Bytheway, B. (1995). *Ageism*. Buckingham: Open University Press.

Carlen, P. (1983). *Women's Imprisonment: A Study in Social Control*. London: Routledge & Keegan Paul.

Carlen, P. (1998). *Sledgehammer: Women's Imprisonment at the Millennium*. Basingstoke: Macmillan Press Ltd.

Carpy, D.V. (1989). 'Tolerating the counter-transference: a mutative process'. *International Journal of Psycho-Analysis*, 70: 287–94.

Carrado, M., George, M.J., Loxam, E., Jones, L. & Templar, D. (1996). 'Aggression in British Heterosexual Relationships: A Descriptive Analysis'. *Aggressive Behaviour*, 22: 401–415.

Central Statistics Office (2002). Dublin: The Stationery Office.

Central Statistics Office (2003). Dublin: The Stationery Office.

Central Statistics Office (2006). Dublin: The Stationery Office.

Central Statistics Office (2007). Dublin: The Stationery Office.

Chance, F. & Halligan, F. (2005). 'Involving fathers in family support: A practice tool'. Dublin: Barnardos. www.barnardos.ie/publications, accessed on 04-08.

Charleton, M. (2007). *Ethics for Social Care in Ireland: Philosophy & Practice*. Dublin: Gill & Macmillan.

Cheal, D. (2002). *Sociology of Family Life*. Hampshire: Palgrave.

Children's Rights Alliance (2008). 'Children's Rights Alliance Submission on the Immigration, Residency and Protection Bill 2008'. Dublin: Children's Rights Alliance.

Citizens Information Board. Retrieved from www.citizensinformation board.ie/services/advocacy_services/, accessed on 27-06-08.

Cleaver, H., Unell, I. & Aldgate, J. (1999). *Children's Needs: Parenting Capacity and the Impact of Parental Mental Illness, Problem Alcohol and Drug Use and Domestic Violence on Children's Development*. London: The Stationery Office.

Clifford, D. & Burke, B. (2005). 'Developing anti-oppressive ethics in the new curriculum'. *Social Work Education*, 24, 6: 677–92.

Coakley, D. (2003). 'Optimising Opportunities for Health and Social Gain in Old Age: The Case for a Concentrated Programme of Health Promotion for Older People'. In: Y. McGivern (2003). Healthy Ageing Conference: Conference Proceedings, Report No. 80. Dublin: NCAOP.

Cohen, S. (2002). *Folk Devils and Moral Panic*. (First published in 1972 by MacGibbon and Kee Ltd) London: Routledge.

Coleman, J. (1972). *On Equality of Education Opportunity*. Washington, DC: Government Printing Office.

Coleman, J. (1988). 'Social Capital in the Creation of Human Capital'. *American Journal of Sociology*, 94 Supplement: S95-S120.

Combat Poverty Agency (2005). 'Disability, Exclusion and Society: Poverty Briefing No. 4'. Dublin: CPA.

Combat Poverty Agency (2006). 'Lone Parent Families and Poverty'. Dublin: CPA.

Conroy, P. (2003). 'Trafficking in Unaccompanied Minors in the European Union Member States – Ireland'. Dublin: International Organisation of Migration.

Convention on the Elimination of All Forms of Discrimination Against Women (CEADW) (1979). General Assembly of the United Nations.

Cooper, J. & Vetere, A. (2005). *Domestic Violence and Family Safety: A Systemic Approach to Working with Violence in Families.* London: Wiley.

Corcoran, M. (2005). 'Portrait of the "Absent" Father: The Impact of Non-residency on Developing and Maintaining a Fathering Role'. *Irish Journal of Sociology,* 14, 2: 134–54.

Corcoran, M. (1999). 'Standards and criteria for the inspection of children's residential homes: the challenges of interdisciplinary co-working'. *Irish Social Worker,* 17: 10.

Corker, M. (1998). 'A proud label: exploring the relationship between disability politics and gay pride'. *Disability and Society,* 9, 3: 343–57.

Corker, M. & French, S. (Eds) (1999). *Disability Discourse.* Buckingham: Open University Press.

Craig, Y. J. (Ed.) (1998). *Advocacy, Counselling and Mediation in Casework.* London: Jessica Kingsley.

Craig, S., Donnellan, M., Graham, G. & Warren, A. (1998). 'Learn to listen'. Dublin: Centre for Social & Educational Research.

Currer, C. (2007). *Loss and Social Work.* Exeter: Learning Matters.

Cussen, D. (2005). 'The Good Life: Ethics and Social Care'. In: P. Share & N. McElwee (Eds). *Applied Social Care: An Introduction for Irish Students.* Dublin: Gill & Macmillan.

Dale, N. (1997). *Working with Families of Children with Special Needs – Partnership and Practice.* London: Routledge.

Dalrymple, J. & Burke, B. (2006). *Anti-Oppressive Practice: Social Care and the Law.* Maidenhead: Open University Press.

Daly, M. & O'Connor, J. (1984). 'The World of the Elderly. The Rural Experience: A study of the elderly person's experience of living alone in a rural area'. Dublin: National Council for the Aged.

Davidson, J. C. (2005). 'Professional relationship boundaries: A social work teaching module'. *Social Work Education,* 24, 5: 511–33.

Davies, C. (2003). 'Workers, Professions and Identity'. In: J. Henderson & D. Atkinson (Eds). *Managing Care in Context.* London: Routledge.

Dennehy, T. (2006). 'Winnicott and the care worker'. In: T. O'Connor & M. Murphy (Eds). *Social Care in Ireland: Theory, Policy and Practice.* Cork: CIT Press.

de Róiste, Á. (2006). 'The Family: A Systems Perspective'. In T. O'Connor & M. Murphy (Eds) *Social Care: Theory, Policy and Practice*. Cork: CIT Press.

Department of Health (1996). 'Interim report of the Joint Committee on the Family'. Dublin: The Stationery Office.

Department of Health (1996). 'Report on the Inquiry into the Operation of Madonna House'. Dublin: The Stationery Office.

Department of Health and Children (1999). 'Children First: National Guidelines for the Protection and Welfare of Children'. Dublin: The Stationery Office.

Department of Health and Children (2007). 'The Agenda for Children's Services: A Policy Handbook'. Dublin: The Stationery Office.

Department of Justice, Equality & Law Reform (2008). 'The National Action Plan Against Racism'. Dublin: The Stationery Office.

Deverell, K. & Sharma, U. (2000). 'Professionalism in everyday practice: issues of trust, experience and boundaries.' In N. Malin (Ed.) *Professionalism, Boundaries and the Workplace*. London: Routledge.

Doyle, M. & Timonen, V. (2007). *Home Care for Ageing Populations: A Comparative Analysis of Domiciliary Care in Denmark, the United States and Germany*. Cheltenham: Edward Elgar.

Dunst, C., Trivette, C. & Deal, A. (1988). *Enabling and Empowering Families: Principles and Guidelines for Practice*. New York: Basic Books.

Durkheim, E. (1933, originally published in 1894). *The Division of Labor in Society*. Translated by George Simpson. New York: The Free Press.

Egan, G. (1994). *The Skilled Helper*. California: Brooks/Cole Publishing Company.

Ellsberg, M. & Heise, L. (2005). *Researching Violence Against Women: A Practical Guide for Researchers and Activists*. Geneva. World Health Organisation.

Elson, M. (1988). *Self Psychology in Clinical Social Work*. New York: W.W. Norton.

Enable Ireland (2008). 'Social and Medical Models of Disability'. Retrieved from http://www.enableireland.ie/at/socialmodel.html, accessed on 01-10-08.

Erikson, E. (1986). *A Way of Looking at Things: Selected Papers from 1930-1986*. London: W.W. Norton.

Fahlberg, V. (1991). *A Child's Journey through Placement*. London: British Agencies for Fostering and Adoption.

Faith, K. (1993). *Unruly Women: The Politics of Confinement and Resistance*. Vancouver: Press Gang Publishers.

Fanning, B. & Rush, M. (Eds) (2006). *Care and Social Change in the Irish Welfare Economy*. Dublin: UCD Press.

Farhall, J. (2001). 'Clinical Psychology and the common good'. *Australasian Psychiatry*, 9, 2: 139–42.

Ferguson, H. & Hogan, F. (2004). 'Strengthening Families through Fathers: Developing Policy and Practice in Relation to Vulnerable Fathers and their Families'. Waterford: Centre for Social and Family Research, WIT. Cited in: K. Lalor, Á. de Róiste & M. Devlin (2007). *Young People in Contemporary Ireland*. Dublin: Gill & Macmillan.

Field, J. (2003). *Social Capital*. London: Routledge.

Finucane, P., Tieman, J. & Moane, G. (1994). 'Support Services for Carers of Elderly People Living At Home'. Retrieved from www.ncaop.ie/publications/research/reports/Support_Services40.pdf, accessed on 12-02-07.

Finnerty & Collins (2005). In: P. Share & N. McElwee (Eds) *Applied Social Care: An Introduction for Irish Students*. Dublin: Gill & MacMillan, p.278.

Flaskas, C. (2005). 'Psychoanalytic ideas and systemic therapy: revising the question "why bother?"'. *Australian and New Zealand Journal of Family Therapy*, 26, 3: 125–34.

Flehkog, M. G. & Kaufman, N. H. (1997). *Rights and Responsibilities in Family and Society*. London: Jessica Kingsley.

Frost, N., Robinson, M. & Anning, A. (2005). 'Social workers in multidisciplinary teams: Issues and dilemmas for professional practice'. *Child and Family Social Work*, 10: 187–96.

Gallagher, C. & O'Toole, J. (1999). 'Towards a sociological understanding of care work in Ireland'. *Irish Journal of Social Work Research*, 2, 1: 60–86.

Garafat, T. (2005). In: P. Share & N. McElwee (Eds) *Applied Social Care: An Introduction for Irish Students*. Dublin: Gill & MacMillan.

Gannon, B. & Nolan, B. (2006). 'The Dynamics of Disability and Social Inclusion'. Dublin: The Equality Authority and National Disability Authority.

Garavan, R., Winder, R. & McGee, H. (2001). 'Health and Social Services for Older People'. Dublin: NCAOP.

Garcia-Moreno, C. (2004). 'Impacts of violence on women's health: A global perspective'. Casualties of Violence – Violence Against Women:

An Issue of Health. Conference Papers. Women's Aid/Department of
Health and Children. www.womensaid.ie, accessed on 05-08.

Gelles, R. (1983). 'An Exchange/Social Control Theory.' In: D.
Finkelhor, R. J. Gelles, G. T. Totaling & M. A. Straus (Eds), *The Dark
Side of Families: Current Family Violence Research*, pp. 151–65. Beverly
Hills: Sage.

Gelles, R. (1997). *Intimate Violence in Families*. London: Sage.

Genders, E. & Player, E. (1987). 'Women in Prison: the Treatment, the
Control and the Experience'. In: P. Carlen & A. Worrall, *Gender,
Crime and Justice*. Milton Keynes: Open University.

Genders, E. & Player, E. (1988). 'Women Lifers: Assessing the
Experience'. In: A. Morris & C. Wilkinson (Eds) *Women and the
Penal System*. Cambridge: Cambridge Institute of Criminology.

Gibson, R. C. (1995). 'Promoting successful and productive aging in
minority populations'. In: L.A. Bond, S.J. Cutler & A. Grams (Eds).
Promoting Successful and Productive Aging, pp. 279–88. Thousand
Oaks, CA: Sage.

Giddens, A. (1992). *The Transformation of Intimacy*. Stanford, CA:
Stanford University Press.

Giddens, A. (2001). *Sociology*. Bristol: Polity Press.

Gil, E. (1982). 'Institutional abuse of children in out-of-home care'.
Child and Youth Care Review, 4, 1–2: 7–13.

Gil, E., cited in Department of Health (1996). Report on the Inquiry
into the Operation of Madonna House. Dublin: The Stationery
Office.

Gilchrist, E., Johnson, R., Takriti, R., Weston, S., Beech, A. & Kebbell,
M. (2003). *Domestic violence offenders: characteristics and offending
related needs*. London: HMSO.

Gilligan, R. (1997). 'Beyond permanence? the importance of resilience in
child placement practice and planning'. *Adoption and Fostering*, 21
(1), 12-20.

Gillon, R. (1992). *Philosophical Medical Ethics*. West Sussex: Wiley.

Girshick, L.B. (1999). *No Safe Haven: Stories of Women in Prison*.
Boston, North Eastern University Press.

Glasby, J. & Dickinson, H. (2008). *Partnership Working in Health and
Social Care*. London: Policy Press.

Goldstein, H. (2001). *Experiential Learning: A Foundation for Social
Work Education and Practice*. Alexandria, VA: Council on Social Work
Education.

Government of Ireland (2001). 'The Youthwork Act'. Dublin: The Stationery Office.

Government of Ireland (2006). The Irish Census. Dublin: The Stationery Office.

Government of Ireland (2007). 'National Action Plan for Social Inclusion 2007-2016'. Dublin: The Stationery Office.

Government of Ireland, Adoption Act 1988, Irish Statute Book, Acts of the Oireachtas, Office of the Attorney General. [www.irishstatutebook.ie/plweb-cgi/fastweb?state_id=1231758331& view=ag-view&numhitsfound=1&query_rule=%28%28$query 3%29%29%3Alegtitle&query3=Adoption%20Act%201988&docid=44 769&docdb=Acts&dbname=Acts&dbname=SIs&sorting=none&oper ator=and&TemplateName=predoc.tmpl&setCookie=1, accessed on 09-10-08.]

Government of Ireland, Child Care Act 1991, Irish Statute Book, Acts of the Oireachtas, Office of the Attorney General. [www.irishstatutebook.ie/plweb-cgi/fastweb?state_id= 1231758496&view=ag-view&numhitsfound=11&query_rule= %28%28$query3%29%29%3Alegtitle&query3=Child%20Care%20Act% 201991&docid=47243&docdb=Acts&dbname=Acts&dbname=SIs&s orting=none&operator=and&TemplateName=predoc.tmpl&setCooki e=1, accessed on 09-10-08.]

Government of Ireland, Domestic Violence Act 1996, Irish Statute Book, Acts of the Oireachtas, Office of the Attorney General. [www.irishstatutebook.ie/plweb-cgi/fastweb?state_id= 1231758574&view=ag-view&numhitsfound=2&query_rule= %28%28$query3%29%29%3Alegtitle&query3=Domestic%20Violence %20Act%201996&docid=52278&docdb=Acts&dbname=Acts&dbna me=SIs&sorting=none&operator=and&TemplateName=predoc.tmpl &setCookie=1, accessed on 09-10-08.]

Government of Ireland, Status of Children Act 1987, Irish Statute Book, Acts of the Oireachtas, Office of the Attorney General. [www.irishstatutebook.ie/plweb-cgi/fastweb?state_id= 1231758209&view=ag-view&numhitsfound=2&query_rule=% 28%28$query3%29%29%3Alegtitle&query3=Status%20of%20Children %20Act%201987&docid=43653&docdb=Acts&dbname=Acts&dbna me=SIs&sorting=none&operator=and&TemplateName=predoc.tmpl &setCookie=1, accessed on 09-10-08.]

Halpern, D. (2005). *Social Capital*. Cambridge: Polity Press.

Hands, M. & Dear, G. (1994). 'Codependency: A critical review'. *Drug and Alcohol Review*, 13: 437–45.

Hardy, B., Turrell, A. & Wistow, G. (1992). *Innovations in Community Care Management*. Aldershot: Avebury.

Hargie, O. (Ed.) (2007). *The Handbook of Communication Skills*. London: Routledge.

Hargie, O., Saunders, C. & Dickson, D. (1996). *Social Skills in Interpersonal Communication*. London: Routledge.

Hartley, P. (Ed.) (2005). *Enhancing Teaching in Higher Education*. London: Routledge.

Hawkins P. & Shohet, R. (1998). *Supervision in the Helping Professions*. Milton Keynes: Open University Press.

Hawkins, P. & Shohet, R. (2002, 2nd Ed.). *Supervision in the Helping Professions*. Milton Keynes. Open University Press.

Health Research Board Trends in problem drug use in Ireland 2001-2006. www.hrb.ie/about/media/media-archives/press-release/release/103/, accessed on 05-08.

Hester, M., Pearson, C. & Harwin, N. (2000). *Making an Impact: Children and Domestic Violence*. London: Jessica Kingsley.

Hirschi, T. (1969). *Causes of Delinquency*. Berkeley: University of California Press.

Hogan, F. & O'Reilly, M. (2007). 'Listening to children: Children's stories of domestic violence'. Dublin: Office of the Minister for Children.

Holt, S. (2003). 'Child protection social work and men's abuse of women: An Irish study'. *Child and Family Social Work*, 8: 53–65.

Huczynski, A. & Buchanan, D. (1991). *Organisational Behaviour: An Introductory Text*. Harlow: FT/Prentice Hall.

Hunter, M. (2001). *Psychotherapy with Young People in Care*. Sussex: Brunner-Routledge.

Irish Prison Service (2006). Annual report. http://irishprisons.ie/documents/IPS-_Annual, accessed on 06-08.

Irish Society for the Prevention of Cruelty to Children (2005). 'Citizen Child Strategy 2005'. Dublin: ISPCC.

IASCE (2005). 'Social Care' (information brochure). Longford: Irish Association of Social Care Educators.

Irish Social Services Inspectorate (2006). 'The management of behaviour: Key lessons from the inspection of high support units'. www.higa.ie, accessed on 05-08.

James, A. (1994). *Managing to Care*. London: Longman.

Jenkins, M. (2003). 'The role of ethics in psychological practice in Ireland'. *Irish Journal of Psychology*, 24, 3–4,184–92.

Jensen, J. & Phillips, S.D. (1996). 'Regime shift: new citizenship practices in Canada'. *International Journal of Canadian Studies*, 14: 111–36.

Jones, P. (2003). *Introducing Social Theory*. Cambridge: Polity Press.

Jones, A.C. (2005). 'Transference, counter-transference and repetition: some implications for nursing practice'. *Journal of Clinical Nursing*, 14: 1177–84.

Jowitt, M. & O'Loughlin, S. (2005). *Social Work with Children and Families*. Exeter: Learning Matters.

Kazdin, A. (1995). *Conduct Disorder in Childhood and Adolescence*. London: Sage.

Keavey, M.E. & Zauszniewski, J.A. (1999). 'Life Events and Psychological Well-Being in Women Sentenced to Prison'. *Issues in Mental Health Nursing*, 20, 1: 73–89.

Kelleher Associates (2001). 'A Framework for Developing an Effective Response to Women and Children Who Experience Male Violence in the Eastern Region'. Dublin: Eastern Regional Planning Committee on Violence Against Women.

Kelleher, P. & O'Connor, M. (1995). 'Making the Links'. Dublin: Women's Aid.

Kelleher, P. & O'Connor, M. (1999). 'Safety and Sanctions: Domestic Violence and the Enforcement of the Law in Ireland'. Dublin: Women's Aid.

Kelly, F., Kelly, C. & Craig, S. (2007). Annual Report of the National Intellectual Disability Database Committee 2007. Dublin: Health Research Board.

Kennefick, P. (2003). 'Training the person: Personal development for care workers'. *European Journal of Social Education*, 4, 91–4.

Kennefick, P. (2006a). 'Phenomenology: A Short Note on a Fundamental Concept'. In: T. O'Connor & M. Murphy (Eds). *Social Care in Ireland: Theory, Policy and Practice*. Cork: CIT Press.

Kennefick, P. (2006b). 'Aspects of Personal Development'. In: T. O'Connor & M. Murphy (Eds). *Social Care in Ireland: Theory, Policy and Practice*. Cork: CIT Press.

Kenny, G. (2004). 'Adjusting to Transitions in Later Life: The Importance of Information for Successful Ageing'. In: J. Heuston (Ed.). *Meeting the Health, Social Care and Welfare Services*

Information Needs of Older People in Ireland. Conference Proceedings, Report No. 78. Dublin: NCAOP.

Kolb, D.A. (1984). *Experiential Learning: Experience as the Source of Learning and Development.* Englewood Cliffs, NJ: Prentice Hall.

Kruttschnitt, C., Gartner, R., et al. (2000). 'Doing Her Own Time: Women's Responses to Prison in the Context of the Old and the New Penology'. *Criminology*, 38, 3: 681–717.

Kubler-Ross, E. (1970). *On Death and Dying.* London: Tavistock.

Kymlinka, W. & Norman, W. (1995). 'Return of the citizen: a survey of recent work on citizenship theory'. In: R. Beiner (Ed.) *Theorizing Citizenship.* Albany, NY: State University of New York Press, pp. 283–322.

Layne, A. Prest, M.J., Benson, H. & Protinsky, O. (1998). 'Family of Origin and Current Relationship Influences on Codependency'. *Family Process*, 37, 4: 523–8.

Layte, R., Fahey, T. & Whelan, C. (1999). 'Income, Deprivation and Well-Being Among Older Irish People'. Dublin: NCAOP.

Lee, P. (1999). Partnership: what does it mean? *Journal of Child Health Care*, 3, 4, 28-32.

Levitas, R. (2005). *The Inclusive Society: Social Exclusion and New Labour.* Basingstoke: Macmillan.

Lewis Herman, J. (1992). *Trauma and Recovery: From Domestic Abuse to Political Terror.* London: Pandora.

Liebling, A. (1994). 'Suicide Amongst Women Prisoners'. *The Howard Journal*, 33, 1: 109.

Lishman, J. (1994). *Communication in Social Work.* London: Macmillan.

Luddy, G. (2003). Paper presented at 'Older Women, Including those Living Alone' (Workshop 4). In Y. McGivern (2003). 2003 Healthy Ageing Conference: Conference Proceedings, Report No. 80. Dublin: NCAOP.

Lum, D. (2004). *Social Work Practice and People of Colour: A Process-stage Approach.* Pacific Grove, CA: Brooks/Cole Publishing Company.

Lustbader, W. (1995). *Counting on Kindness: The Dilemmas of Dependency.* New York: Free Press.

Lynch, K. (1989). 'Solidary Labour: Its Nature and Marginalisation', *Sociological Review*, 37: 1–14.

Lynch, K. & McLaughlin, E. (1995). 'Caring Labour and Love Labour'. In: P. Clancy et al. (Eds). 'Irish Society: Sociological Perspectives'.

Dublin: Institute of Public Administration. pp. 250-92.

Lynch, K., Lyons, M. & Feeley, M. (2006). 'Rationalities of Care: Care as the antithesis of the "rational economic man" thesis'. Paper presented at 'Equality and social Inclusion in the 21st Century: Developing Alternatives Conference', Belfast, 1–3 February 2006.

MacDonald, R. & Marsh, J. (2000). 'Employment, Unemployment and Social Polarization'. In: R. Crompton, et al. *Renewing Class Analysis*. Oxford: Blackwell.

MacDonald, C. (2006). *Challenging Social Work: The Institutional Context of Practice*. Houndmills: Palgrave.

Macionis, J. & Plummer, K. (2002, 2nd Ed.). *Sociology: A Global Introduction*. London: Prentice Hall.

Mantell, A. & Scraggs, T. (Eds) (2008). *Safeguarding Adults in Social Work*. Exeter: Learning Matters.

March, P. & Doherty, C. (2001). 'Dying and bereavement'. In: D. Messer & F. Jones (Eds). *Psychology and Social Care*, 489–504. London: Jessica Kingsley.

Marshall, T. H. (1963). *Sociology at the Crossroads and Other Essays*. London: Heinemann.

Martin. V. & Henderson, E. (2001). *Managing in Health and Social Care*. Routledge: Open University Press.

Maslow, A. (1943). 'A Theory of Human Motivation'. *Psychological Review*, 50, 370-396.

Matthews, R. (1999). *Doing Time: An Introduction to the Sociology of Imprisonment*. London: MacMillan Press Ltd.

Mayock, P. & Carr, N. (2008). 'Not just homelessness… A study of "out of home" young people in Cork city'. Dublin: Children's Research Centre/HSE.

McCann, C. (1995). *Who Cares? A Guide for All who Care for Others*. Dublin. Columba Press.

McCann James, C. (2001). 'Recycled Women: Oppression and the Social World of Women Prisoners in the Irish Republic'. Unpublished PhD dissertation, NUI, Galway.

McCann James, C. (2004). 'Motherhood Adjourned: The Experience of Mothers in Prison'. In: P. Kennedy, (Ed.). *Motherhood in Ireland: Creation and Context*. Cork: Mercier Press.

McCann James, C. (2005). 'Ethnicity and Social Care: An Irish Dilemma'. In P. Share & N. McElwee (Eds). *Applied Social Care: An Introduction for Irish Students*. Dublin: Gill & Macmillan.

McCarthy, B., Hagan, J. & Martin, M. (2002). 'In and Out of Harm's Way: Violent Victimization and the Social Capital of Fictive Street Families'. *Criminology*, 40, 4: 831–65.

McDonald, B. (2006). *An Introduction to Sociology in Ireland*. Dublin: Gill & Macmillan.

McGarty, P. (2005). 'Leadership and teamwork in social care'. In: P. Share & N. McElwee (Eds). *Applied Social Care: An Introduction for Irish Students*. Dublin: Gill & Macmillan.

McGivern, Y. (Ed.) (2003). Healthy Ageing Conference: Conference Proceedings Report No. 80. Dublin: NCAOP. Retrieved from www.ncaop.ie/publications/research/reports/80_HA_2003Conf.pdf , accessed on 12-02-07.

McKay, S. (1998). *Sophia's Story*. Dublin: Gill & Macmillan.

McKenna-McElwee, S. & Brown, T. (2005). 'Community childcare'. In: P. Share & N. McElwee (Eds) *Applied Social Care: An Introduction for Irish Students*. Dublin: Gill & Macmillan.

McKeown, K. Ferguson, H. & Rooney, D. (1998*). Changing Fathers? Fathers and Family Life in Ireland*. Cork: Collins Press.

McKeown, K., Haase, T. & Pratschke, J. (2001). 'Springboard: Promoting family well-being through family support services'. Dublin: Department of Health and Children.

McKeown, K. & Kidd, P. (2000). 'Men and Domestic Violence: What Research Tells Us'. Dublin: Department of Health and Children.

McKeown, K., Pratschke, J., & Haase, T. (2003). 'Family Well-Being: What Makes a Difference?' Report to the Ceifin Centre, Co. Clare. Retrieved from www.welfare.ie/publications/famwelloct03.pdf, accessed on 01-07-08.

McKiernan F. (1996). 'Bereavement and attitudes to death'. In: R.T. Woods (Ed.), *Handbook of the Clinical Psychology of Ageing*. New York: Wiley & Sons, pp.159–181.

McWilliams, A. (2006). 'The Challenges of Working Together in Child Protection'. In: T. O'Connor & M. Murphy (Eds). *Social Care in Ireland: Theory, Policy and Practice*. Cork: CIT Press.

Meenan, D. (2005). 'Working in social care'. In: P. Share & N. McElwee (Eds). *Applied Social Care: An Introduction for Irish Students*. Dublin: Gill & Macmillan.

Merritt, C. (1980). 'Emotional First Aid'. *The Pointer*, 25, 2: 16–25.

Merton, R. (1957). *Social Theory and Social Structure*. New York: Free Press of Glencoe.

Mikulincer, M. & Shaver, P.R. (2005). 'Attachment security, compassion and altruism'. *Current Directions in Psychological Science*, 14: 34–8.

Miley, K.K., O'Melia, M. & DuBois, B. (2004). *Generalist Social Work Practice: An Empowering Approach.* Boston: Pearson.

Mills, S. (2002). *Clinical Practice and the Law.* Dublin: Butterworths.

Minuchin, P. (2002). 'Looking toward the horizon: Present and future in the study of family systems'. In: J. McHale & W. Grolnick (Eds). *Retrospect and Prospect in the Psychological Study of Families*, 259–78. NJ: Lawrence Erlbaum Assoc.

Moore, Wilbert, E. (1970). *The Professions: Roles and Rules.* New York: Russell Sage Foundation.

Mooten, N. (2006). 'Making Separated Children Visible: The Need for a Child Centred Approach'. Dublin: Irish Refugee Council.

Moran, M. (2006). 'Social Inclusion and the Limits of Pragmatic Liberalism: The Irish Case'. *Irish Political Studies*, 21, 2: 181–201.

Morley, M., Moore, S., Heraty, N. & Gunnigle, P. (1998). *Principles of Organizational Behaviour: An Irish Text.* Dublin: Gill & Macmillan.

Morrell, P. (1999). 'The professionalisation of social care in Ireland?' In: P. Share & N. McElwee (Eds). *Applied Social Care: An Introduction for Irish Students.* Dublin: Gill & Macmillan.

Mueller, F., Procter, S. & Buchanan, D. (2000). Teamworking in its context(s): Antecedents, nature and dimensions. *Human Relations*, 53, 11, pp. 1387-1424.

Murgatroyd, S. (1996). *Counselling and Helping.* Leicester: BPS Books.

Murphy, P.M. & Kupshik, G.A. (1992). *Loneliness, Stress and Well-Being: A Helper's Guide.* London: Routledge.

Murray, C. (1984). *Losing Ground: American Social Policy, 1950-1980.* New York: Basic Books.

Murray, C. (2006). 'In Our Hands: A Plan to Replace the Welfare State'. Washington DC: American Enterprise Institute for Public Policy Research.

National Council for the Aged (1985). Dublin. Retrieved from www.ncaop.ie/publications/research/intros/intro_11_Institutional.pdf, accessed on 12-02-07.

National Council on Ageing and Older People (2004). 'Loneliness and Social Isolation Among Older Irish People'. Dublin: NCAOP.

National Council on Ageing and Older People (2005). 'An Age Friendly Society: A Position Paper'. Dublin: NCAOP.

National Council for Aging and Older People (2005). www.ncaop.ie, accessed on 09-05-08.

National Crime Council/ESRI (2005). 'Domestic abuse of women and men in Ireland: Report of the national study of domestic abuse'. Dublin: NCC/ESRI.

National Health Service (NHS) (2007). 'Policy for Personal and Professional Boundaries'. Retrieved from www.newforestpct.nhs.uk/foi/hrpolicies/4.pdf, accessed on 01-07-08.

National Intellectual Disability Database (2008). Annual Report of the National Intellectual Disability Database Committee 2007. Dublin: Health Research Board.

Neimeyer, R. (2001). *Meaning Reconstruction and the Experience of Loss.* Washington DC: American Psychological Association.

Nelson-Jones, R. (1993). *Practical Counseling and Helping Skills.* London: Cassell.

Nies, H. & Berman, P. (Eds) (2007). *Integrating Services for Older People: A Resource Book for Managers.* Dublin: EHMA.

Nixon, E., Greene, S. & Hogan, D. (2006). 'Concepts of family among children and young people in Ireland. *Irish Journal of Psychology*, 27, 1–2: 79–87.

Nolan, M. (1995). 'Towards an ethos of interdisciplinary practice'. *British Medical Journal*, 311: 305–6.

Obholzer, A. & Roberts, V.Z. (Eds) (2005). *The Unconscious at Work: Individual and Organisational Stress in the Human Services.* London: Routledge.

O'Brien, J. and Lyle O'Brien, C. (1998). *A Little Book about Person Centered Planning.* Toronto: Inclusion Press.

O'Brien, J. (1989). What's Worth Working For? Leadership for Better Quality Human Services. http://soeweb.syr.edu/thechp/rsapub.htm.

O'Carroll, J. (1998). 'Blood'. In: M. Peillon & E. Slater (Eds), *Encounters with Modern Ireland.* Dublin: Institute of Public Administration.

O'Connor, M. (2004). 'Violence Against Women: The Response of the Health System in Ireland'. In: Casualties of Violence, Conference Papers. Dublin: Women's Aid.

O'Connor, P. (1998). *Emerging Voices: Women in Contemporary Irish Society.* Dublin: Institute of Public Administration.

O'Connor, T. & Murphy, M. (2006*). Social Care in Ireland: Theory, Policy and Practice.* Cork: CIT Press.

O'Connor, M. & Wilson, N. (2002). Vision Action Change: Feminist Principles and Practice of Working on Violence Against Women. Dublin: Women's Aid. www.womensaid.ie, accessed on 06-08.

O'Doherty, C. (2005). 'Integrating Social Care and Social Work: Towards a Model of Best Practice'. In: P. Share & N. McElwee (Eds), *Applied Social Care: An Introduction for Irish Students*. Dublin: Gill & Macmillan.

O'Doherty, C. (2007). *A New Agenda for Family Support: Providing Services that Create Social Capital*. London: Blackhall.

O'Farrell, H. (1999). *First Steps in Counselling*. Dublin: Veritas.

O'Ferrall, F. (2002). *The Future Is Ours: Be the Change*. Dublin: The Wheel.

O'Hagan, K. & Dillenberger, K. (1995). *The Abuse of Women in Childcare Work*. Buckingham: Open University Press.

Office of the United Nations High Commissioner for Human Rights (OHCHR) (1949). *Convention for the Suppression of the Traffic in Persons and of the Exploitation of the Prostitution of Others*. Geneva, Switzerland.

Office of the United Nations High Commissioner for Human Rights (OHCHR) (1993). *Declaration on Elimination of Violence against Women*. Geneva, Switzerland.

Oliver, M. (1990). *The Politics of Disablement*. London: Macmillan.

Oliver, M. (1996). 'Defining impairment and disability: issues at stake'. In: C. Barnes & G. Mercer (Eds). *Exploring the Divide: Illness and Disability*. Leeds: Disability Press, pp. 139–54.

O'Moore, A.M., Kirkham, C. & Smith, M. (1997). 'Bullying behaviour in Irish schools'. *Aggressive Behaviour*, 26: 99–111.

O'Neill, E. (2003). 'Using Professional Supervision in Social Care'. In: P. Share & N. McElwee (Eds), *Applied Social Care: An Introduction for Irish Students*. Dublin: Gill & Macmillan.

O'Neill, E. (2004). *Professional Supervision: Myths, Culture and Structure*. Tipperary, Ireland: RMA Publications.

O'Shea, E. (2003). 'Healthy Ageing in Ireland: Policy Practice and Evaluation'. Dublin: NCAOP.

O'Shea, E. & Connolly, S. (2003). Healthy Ageing in Ireland: Policy, Practice and Evaluation. Proceedings of the Healthy Aging Conference. www.ncaop.ie.

Olweus, D. (1992). 'Bullying among school children: Intervention and prevention'. In: R.D. Peters, R.J. McMahon & V.L. Quincy (Eds),

Aggression and Violence Throughout the Life-Span. Thousand Oaks, CA: Sage Publications.

Olweus, D. (1992). 'Victimisation by peers: antecedents and long term outcomes'. In: K.H. Rubin & J.B. Asendorf (Eds), *Social Withdrawal, Inhibition and Shyness in Children*. Hillsdale, NJ: Erlbaum.

Osterman & Kottkamp (1993). 'Rethinking Professional Development'. In: N. Bennet, R. Glatter & Levacic (Eds) (1994). *Improving Educational Management Through Research and Consultancy*. Milton Keynes: PCP.

Øvretveit (1995). 'Team decision-making'. *Journal of Interprofessional Care*, 9, 1, pp. 41-51.

Owen, B. (1999). 'Women and Imprisonment in the United States: The Gendered Consequences of the US Imprisonment Binge'. In: S. Cook & S. Davies (Eds), *Harsh Punishment: International Experiences of Women's Imprisonment*. Boston: North Eastern University Press.

Parkes, C.M. & Weiss, R.S. (1983). *Recovery for Bereavement*. New York: Basic Books.

Parsons, T. (1971). 'The Normal American Family'. In: B. Adams & T. Weirath (Eds), *Readings on the Sociology of the Family*. Chicago: Markham.

Payne, M. (1997) *Modern Social Work Theory*. London: Macmillan.

Peillon, M. (1998). 'Community of Distrust'. In: M. Peillon & E. Slater (Eds). *Encounters with Modern Ireland*. Dublin: Institute of Public Administration.

Pelchat D. & Lefebvre, H. (2004). 'A holistic intervention programme for families with a child with a disability'. *Journal of Advanced Nursing*, 48, 2: 124–31.

Peled, E., Eisikovits, Enosh, G. & Winstok, Z. (2000). 'Choice and empowerment for battered women who stay: toward a constructivist model'. *Social Work*, 45: 9–25.

Pennix, P.R. (1999). 'An Analysis of Mothers in the Federal Prison System'. *Corrections Compendium*, 24, 12: 4–6.

Pervin, L. (1989, 5th Ed.). *Personality: Theory and Research*. New York: Wiley.

Peterson, M.R. (1992). *At Personal Risk: Boundary Violations in Professional-Client Relationships*. New York: W.W. Norton.

Phillips, J. (2001). *Groupwork in Social Care: Planning and Setting up Groups*. London: Jessica Kingsley.

Pierce, M. (2008). 'Constructions of Ageing in Irish Social Policy'. In: P. Kennedy & S. Quin (Eds). *Ageing and Social Policy in Ireland*. Dublin: UCD Press.

Pine, B., Walsh, R. & Maluccio, A. (2003). 'Participatory management in public child welfare agency: a key to effective change'. In: J. Reynolds et al. (Eds). *The Managing Care Reader*. New York: Routledge.

Plummer, K. (1979) 'Misunderstanding Labelling Perspectives'. In: D. Downes & P. Rock (Eds),*Deviant Interpretations*. Oxford: Oxford University Press.

Powell, F. & Guerin, D. (1999). *Civil Society and Active Citizenship: The Role of the Voluntary Sector*. Coleraine: Centre for Voluntary Action Studies.

Prithchard, J. (Ed.) (2001). *Good Practice with Vulnerable Adults*. London: Jessica Kingsley.

Quinn, A. (1999). 'The Use of Experiential Learning to Help Social Work Students Assess Their Attitudes Towards Practice With Older People'. *Social Work Education*, 18, 2: 171–82.

Ramcharan, P., Roberts, G., Grant, G. & Borland, J. (Eds) (2000). *Empowerment in Everyday Life: Learning Disability*. London: Jessica Kingsley.

Rea, A. (2001). Psychosocial needs, social support and estimates of psychological distress among unaccompanied refugee minors in Ireland. Doctoral in Clinical Psychology Thesis, Queen's University, Belfast. Cited in: P. Reder, S. Duncan & M. Gray (1993), *Beyond Blame*. New York: Routledge.

Redl, F. (1959). 'The concept of the life space interview'. *American Journal of Orthopsychiatry*, 29: 1–18.

Redl, F. & Wineman, D. (1952). *Controls from Within: Techniques for the Treatment of the Aggressive Child*. New York: The Free Press.

Richards, M., McWilliams, B., Batten, N. & Cutler, J. (1995). 'Foreign Nationals in English Prisons: Family Ties and their Maintenance'. *The Howard Journal*, 34, 2: 158–75.

Richardson, L. (2003). Paper presented at 'Older Women, Including those Living Alone' (Workshop 4). In: Y. McGivern (Ed.), Healthy Ageing Conference: Conference Proceedings, Report No. 80. Dublin: NCAOP.

Riggio, R.E. (2003, 4th Ed.). *Introduction to Industrial/Organizational Psychology*. New Jersey: Prentice-Hall.

Rioux, M. (2003). 'On Second Thoughts: Constructing Knowledge, Law, Disability and Inequality'. In: S. Herr et al. (Eds), *The Rights of Persons with Intellectual Disability: Different but Equal*. Oxford: Oxford University Press, pp. 287–318.

Robinson, M. (1991). *Family Transformation Through Divorce and Remarriage*. London: Routledge.

Roeher, I. (1993). *Social Well-Being: A Paradigm for Reform*. Toronto: Roeher Institute.

Rogers, C. (1960). *On Becoming a Person*. Boston: Houghton Mifflin.

Rogers, C.R. (1942). *Counseling and Psychotherapy: New Concepts in Practice*. Boston: Houghton Mifflin.

Rook, K.S. (1984). 'Research on social support, loneliness and social isolation'. In: P. Shaver (Ed.), *Review of Personality and Social Psychology*. Beverly Hills: Sage Publications.

Rowe, J.W. & Kahn, R.L. (1987). 'Human ageing: Usual and successful'. *Science*, 237, 4811: 143–9.

Ruddle H., O'Donoghue, F. & Mulvihill, R. (1997). The years ahead report: A review of the implementation of its recommendations. Dublin: National Council on Ageing and Older People.

Ruhama (2007). *Prostitution as So-Called Free Choice*, Discussion Paper. www.ruhama.ie/page. php?intPageID=109.

Ryan, T. & Walker, K. (1993). *Life Story Work*. London: Sage.

Sainsbury Centre for Mental Health, Training and Practice Development Section (2001). 'The Capable Practitioner'. London: Sainsbury Centre for Mental Health.

Sale, A. (2002). 'Codes of conduct promise to rejuvenate social care sector'. *Community Care*, p. 1404.

Salzberger-Wittenberg, I. (1970). *Psycho-Analytic Insight and Relationships: A Klienian Approach*. London: Routledge.

Schön, D.A. (1983). *The Reflective Practitioner: How Professionals Think in Action*. Aldershot: Arena.

Schön, D.A. (1987). *Educating the Reflective Practitioner*. San Francisco: Jossey-Bass.

Seden, J. (2003). 'Managers and their Organisations'. In: J. Henderson & D. Atkinson (Eds). *Managing Care in Context*. London: Routledge.

Seligman, M. (2002). *Authentic Happiness: Using New Positive Psychology to Realize your Potential for Lasting Fulfillment*. New York: Free Press.

Share, P. & McElwee, N. (Eds) (2005) *Applied Social Care*. Dublin: Gill & Macmillan.

Sharrock, W. (1977). 'The Problem of Order'. In: P. Worsley (Ed.), *Introducing Sociology*. Harmondsworth: Penguin.

Shaw, M. (1999). 'Knowledge Without Acknowledgement: Violent Women, the Prison and the Cottage'. *The Howard Journal*, 38, 3: 252–66.

Shiely, F. & Kelleher, C. (2003). The Health and Lifestyle of Older People: Findings from SLÁN 1998 and 2002. In: Y. McGivern (Ed.), Healthy Ageing Conference: Conference Proceedings, Report No. 80. Dublin: NCAOP.

Shildrick, M. & Price, J. (1996). 'Breaking the Boundaries of the Broken Body'. *Body and Society*, 2, 4: 93–113.

Sloper, P. (1999). 'Models of service support for parents of disabled children. What do we know? What do we need to know?'. *Child: Care, Health and Development*, 25: 85–99.

Sociological Association of Ireland (SAI) (2004). Ethical Guidelines for the Association of Ireland. http://www.ucd.ie/sai/SAI_ethics.htm, accessed on 20-11-08.

South Eastern Health Board (1993). Kilkenny Incest Investigation Report. Dublin: The Stationery Office.

Stevenson, O. (1999). *Neglected Children: Issues and Dilemmas*. London: Blackwell.

Stroebe, M. & Schut W. (1995). Cited in: C. Currer (2007). *Loss and Social Work*. Exeter: Learning Matters.

Thomas, C. (1999). *Female Forms: Experiencing and Understanding Disability*. Buckingham: Open University Press.

Thomas, C. (2001). 'Feminism and Disability: The Theoretical and Political Significance of the Personal and the Experiential'. In: L. Barton (Ed), *Disability, Politics and the Struggle for Change*. London: David Fulton Publications, pp. 45–58.

Thomas, C. (2002). 'The "Disabled" Body'. In: M. Evans & E. Lee (Eds), *Real Bodies*. Basingstoke: Macmillan.

Thomas, D. & Woods, H. (2003). *Working with People with Disabilities: Theory and Practice*. London: Jessica Kingsley.

Thomas, K.W. (1976). Conflict and conflict management. In M.D. Dunnette (Ed.), *Handbook of Industrial and Organizational Psychology*. Chicago: Rand McNally, pp. 889–935.

Thompson, N. (1997). *Anti-Oppressive Practice*. London: Macmillan.

Thompson, N. (2002). *People Skills*. Hampshire: Palgrave/Macmillan.

Tovey, H. & Share, P. (2007, 3rd Ed.). *A Sociology of Ireland*. Dublin: Gill & Macmillan.

Treacy. P., Butler. M., Byrne, A., Drennan, J., Fealy, G., Frazer, K. & Irving, K. (2005). 'Loneliness and Social Isolation Among Older Irish People'. Report No. 84. Dublin: NCAOP.

Trotter, C. (1999). *Working with Involuntary Clients*. London: Sage.

Tuckman, B.W. (1965). 'Developmental Sequence in Small Groups'. *Psychological Bulletin*, 63, 1965: 384–99.

UN Centre for Human Rights (1994). *Human Rights and Social Work*. New York: United Nations.

Van Hasselt, V.B., Morrison R.L., Bellack, A.S., Hersen, M. (Eds) (1988). *Handbook of Family Violence*. New York: Plenum.

Veale, A., Palaudaries, L. & Gibbons, C. (2003). 'Separated children seeking asylum in Ireland'. Dublin: Irish Refugee Council.

Vekić, K. (2003). 'Unaccompanied Minors in Ireland: From Understanding to Response'. Dublin: Marino Institute.

Walker, A. (1999). 'Public Policy and Theories of Aging: Constructing and Reconstructing Old Age'. In: V.L. Bengston & K.W. Schaie (Eds), *Handbook of Theories of Aging*. New York: Springer.

Walsh, J., Craig, S. & McCafferty, D. (1998). *Local Partnerships for Social Inclusion*. Dublin: Oak Tree Press.

Wanzenböck, J. (2006). Submission cited in: N. Mooten. 'Making separated children visible: The need for a child centred approach'. Dublin: The Irish Refugee Council.

Ward, A., Kasinski, K., Pooley, J. & Worthington, A. (2003). *Therapeutic Communities for Children and Young People*. London: Jessica Kingsley.

Ward, A. (2008). Beyond the instructional mode: creating a holding environment for learning about the use of self. *Journal of Social Work Practice*, 22, 3, March 2008, pp. 67-83.

Watson, D. & Parsons, S. (2005). *Domestic Violence in Ireland*. National Crime Council with the Economic and Social Research Institute. Dublin: The Stationery Office.

Watson, D., Townsley, R. & Abbott, D. (2002). 'Exploring multi-agency working in services to disabled children with complex healthcare needs and their families'. *Journal of Clinical Nursing*, 11: 367–75.

Weafer, J. & Woods, M. (2003). 'The Jigsaw of Advocacy: Finding a Voice. A research report compiled for Comhairle'. Dublin: Comhairle.

Weber, M. (1978, originally 1921). *Economy and Society*. In: G. Roth & Wittich (Eds). Berkeley, CA: University of California Press.

Weiss, R.S. (1973). *Loneliness: The Experience of Emotional and Social Isolation*. Cambridge: MIT Press.

West, M. (1994). *Effective Teamwork*. Leicester: The British Psychology Society.

Whitfield, C.L. (1987). *Healing the Child Within: Discovery and Recovery for Adult Children of Dysfunctional Families.* Deerfield Beach, FL: Health Communications, Inc.

Wilkins-Shurmer, A., O'Callaghan, M.J., Najman, J.M., Bor, W., Williams, G.M. & Anderson, M.J. (2003). 'Association of bullying with adolescent health-related quality of life'. *Journal of Paediatrics and Child Health*, 39: 436–41.

Williams, D. (2002). *Communication Skills in Practice: A Practical Guide for Health Professionals.* London: Jessica Kingsley.

Wilson, W.J. (1987). *The Truly Disadvantaged.* Chicago: University of Chicago Press.

Wilson, W.J. (1996). *When Work Disappears.* New York: Knopf.

Woliver, L. (1996). 'Mobilizing and Sustaining Grassroots Dissent'. *Journal of Social Issues*, 52, 1: 139–51.

Women's Aid (2006). Statistics Report 2006. Dublin: Women's Aid.

Women's Health Council (2007). Violence Against Women & Health. Dublin: Office of the Minister for Health and Children, The Stationery Office.

Worden, W. (1991, 2nd Ed.). *Grief Counselling and Grief Therapy: A Handbook for the Mental Health Practitioner.* London: Routledge.

Worthington, A. et al. (Eds) (2004). *Therapeutic Communities for Children and Young People.* London: Jessica Kingsley.

www.theworldcafe.com, accessed on 28-10-08.

Young, D.S. & Jefferson Smith, C. (2000). 'When Moms are Incarcerated: The Needs of Children, Mothers and Caregivers'. *Families in Society: The Journal of Contemporary Human Services*, 81, 2: 130–47.

Zimmerman, M.A. (1995). 'Psychological empowerment: Issues and illustrations'. *American Journal of Community Psychology*, 23, 581–99.

Zimmerman, M.A. & Warschausky, S. (1998). 'Empowerment theory for rehabilitation research: Conceptual and methodological issues'. *Rehabilitation Psychology*, 43, 1: 3–16.

Index